ATTRACT MONEY NOW!

How to go from survival to security,
from fear to freedom,
from worry to wealthy,
from victim to victor
in just Seven *Easy* Steps!

BY DR. JOE VITALE
Author of way too many books to list here

LIMIT OF LIABILITY/DISCLAIMER OF WARRANTY:
While the publisher, designers, contributors, editors, and author have used their best efforts in preparing the *Attract Money Now* book, they make no warranties or representations with respect to the accuracy or completeness of the contents of this book and specifically disclaim any implied warranties of merchantability or finances for a particular purpose. It is further acknowledged that no warranty, of any kind, may be created or extended by any written sales materials or sales representatives. **The advice and strategies contained herein may not be suitable for your situation and do contain risk including the risk of financial loss. You should always consult with a financial or legal professional where appropriate before undertaking any action and users of this material assume all risk. Neither the publisher, designers, editors, contributors nor the author shall be liable for any loss of profit or any other commercial damages, including but not limited to financial, special, incidental, consequential, or other damages.**

Copyright © 2010 by Hypnotic Marketing, Inc. All rights reserved. Distribution and reproduction are strictly prohibited by law. It's also bad karma.

Second Edition.

Published by Hypnotic Marketing, Inc., Austin, TX

No part of this publication may be reproduced, stored in a retrieval system, or transmitted in any form, or by any means, electronic, mechanical, photocopying, recorded, scanning, or otherwise, except as permitted under Section 107 or 108 of the 1976 United States Copyright Act, without the prior written permission of the publisher or author. Requests to the author should be addressed to Dr. Joe Vitale's VP of Operations at suzanne@mrfire.com

For information about reprint rights, translation, or bulk purchases, please contact Suzanne Burns at suzanne@mrfire.com. Or you can write to Hypnotic Marketing Inc., P.O. Box 2924, Wimberley TX 78676. Phone 512-278-1610.

Library of Congress Cataloging-in-Publication Data
Vitale, Joseph Gary 1953 –
   Attract Money Now ©

   1. Money. 2. Spirituality. 3. Human Potential. 4. Self-Help. 5. Finance.
   6. Law of Attraction. 7. New Thought. 8. Prosperity.

"I have enjoyed reading and have learned something new and valuable from every one of Joe Vitale's books. Attract Money Now is another solid winner! It is full of profound insights, inspiring stories and practical strategies. I highly recommend it!"
— JACK CANFIELD, CO-AUTHOR OF *CHICKEN SOUP FOR THE SOUL* AND *THE SUCCESS PRINCIPLES*

"Joe Vitale explains in step-by-step fashion how to request, attract, receive, and spend money from a place of abundance instead of scarcity. Filled with powerful distinctions and inspiring stories of both failure and success, this book shares what it takes to go from poverty to wealth and to unleash your full potential as a world-class contributor. Attract Money Now is a valuable resource for any serious seeker of financial abundance."
— STEVE PAVLINA, AUTHOR OF *PERSONAL DEVELOPMENT FOR SMART PEOPLE*

"This page-turner reveals the real secrets to attracting money! I love it!"
— JENNIFER NICOLE LEE, INTERNATIONAL FITNESS CELEBRITY

"Joe Vitale has done it again! Joe's book, Attract Money Now Contains absolutely everything you need to know, along with a clear step-by-step formula to begin attracting money right away. I'm recommending this book to all my clients and friends."
— EVA GREGORY, AUTHOR OF *THE FEEL GOOD GUIDE TO PROSPERITY* AND *LIFE LESSONS FOR MASTERING THE LAW OF ATTRACTION*

FREE MONEY!

Well, not exactly.
But the digital version of this book is available for free.
Read it on-line, use it, and you can attract money now.

**For the e-book version,
please visit** http://www.attractmoneynow.com

> "You are the Michelangelo of your own life.
> The David you are sculpting is you."
>
> — DR. JOE VITALE, IN THE HIT MOVIE *THE SECRET*

ACKNOWLEDGEMENTS

Nobody writes a book entirely alone. Peter Wink, my vice-president of marketing, carefully edited this book, as did Suzanne Burns, my publicist and executive administrator. Dee Burks did the initial research and structure for the book. Many others helped in the process, not the least of whom was Nerissa, my life partner who took care of the critters so I could focus on creating this book. Ted Angel created the cover and book layout. Brian Fitzsimmons took the cover photographs. I have many inner circle supporters in my life, a few include Pat O'Bryan, Craig Perrine, Bill Hibbler, Mark Ryan, Rick and Mary Barrett, and Victoria Belue Schaefer. There's a long list of prosperity teachers who have influenced me, including Rev. Ike, Catherine Ponder, Joseph Murphy, Edwene Gaines, Eric Butterworth, Charles Fillmore, Elizabeth Towne, William Walker Atkinson, Robert Collier, Neville Goddard, Vernon Howard, Stuart Wilde, Terri Cole Whittaker and Bob Proctor. If I've forgotten anyone instrumental in creating this book, please forgive me. I am grateful for all of you, including you, the reader. Without you, this book wouldn't be necessary. Please enjoy it and live long and prosper.

DEDICATION

To Bobby Birdsall

CONTENTS

Author's Amazing Introduction	10
The Optimist Creed	12
Grasping the Golden Ring	13
Step 1: Alter How You Think	27
Step 2: Give Without Expectation	38
Step 3: Prosperous Spending	49
Step 4: Ask for Help	62
Step 5: Nevillize Your Goals	73
Step 6: Think Like an Entrepreneur	84
Step 7: Help Your Community & Your World	96
The Freedom to Live!	108
Afterword: Take Inspired Action NOW!	119
Bonus: 29 Ways to Attract Money Now	120
***Super* Bonus: The Secret to Attract Money Now!**	122
Bonus: A Divine Way to Clear Limiting Beliefs About Money	131
Bibliography	134
Resources	142
Catalog of Products	145
About the Author	155
Special Miracles Coaching™ Offer	160

ATTRACT MONEY NOW!

How to go from survival to security,
from fear to freedom,
from worry to wealthy,
from victim to victor
in just Seven *Easy* Steps!

BY DR. JOE VITALE
Author of way too many books to list here

AUTHOR'S AMAZING INTRODUCTION

Money will match your mindset.
Change your mind and you can attract money now.
— DR. JOE VITALE

IF YOU'VE BEEN STRUGGLING with money, or worried about your job or future, you've come to the right place.

If you've been wondering how to attract more money using things you might have heard about, such as the Law of Attraction, then you've come to the right place.

If you've been confused about how to make money in tough economic times, when the media declares we are in a recession or even depression, then you've come to the right place.

My name is Joe Vitale and I intend to help you attract money now. I don't care who or where you are. I don't care about your education or experience. I don't care if you have a job or a business right now. I care about *you*, without knowing any more than you are ready for change. How do I know? Because you are reading this book. You have signaled that you are ready for help.

I guarantee that I can help you if you take inspired action on what you learn in *Attract Money Now*. I've developed a seven-step formula that will work. All you have to do is read this book and then take action. Yes, it's that simple. If you trust me, and take action, I will help you. You can once and for all leave the struggle behind. You can finally break free from desperation and find a place of peace, prosperity, and happiness.

There are plenty of books and courses on how to buy real estate, invest in stocks or start a business. They all assume you already have money. What if you don't? What if you're truly desperate? What if you're truly broke? What if you're not sure what to do with the little money you may have?

Author's Amazing Introduction

I'm so convinced that my seven-step formula will work for you or anyone else – that I am giving the digital version of this book away for free.

Why am I so confident these seven steps will work?

In the mid-1970s I was homeless. No car. No home. No money. No job. No food. No friends. No hope. I was penniless.

In the late 1970s through the early 1980s I was in poverty. I lived in a room in a house. The toilet was behind a curtain in the living room. It cost me $200 a month to live there and I usually struggled to come up with the money.

Today I'm a bestselling author of dozens of books, have appeared on national television, including *Larry King Live*, am in numerous movies, such as *The Secret* and *The Compass*, and I have many audios, DVDs, home-study courses, as well as my world-famous Miracles Coaching program.

I also have car, guitar, and book collections. I've also given thousands of dollars to complete strangers, started a movement called Operation YES to end homelessness, and work with groups from all over the country to stop poverty.

How did I go from homeless and in poverty to a multi-millionaire celebrity?

How did I create a world-famous Miracles Coaching™ program to help thousands of people?

I used the seven steps revealed in this book. They worked for me. They work for others. They will work for you. If you are ready to experience the change from struggle to security, from worry to wealth, from fear to freedom, then just turn the page.

Expect Miracles!
Dr. Joe Vitale
www.JoeVitale.com

PS: If you know someone who needs help attracting more money, please send them to my website where they can get a free digital copy of this book: http://www.attractmoneynow.com

THE OPTIMIST CREED

ORIGINALLY PUBLISHED IN 1912 in a book titled *Your Forces and How to Use Them*, this famous creed by Christian D. Larson is worth reading every morning and evening.

PROMISE YOURSELF...

To be so strong that nothing can disturb your peace of mind.

To talk health, happiness, and prosperity to every person you meet.

To make all your friends feel that there is something worthwhile in them.

To look at the sunny side of everything and make your optimism come true.

To think only of the best, to work only for the best and to expect only the best.

To be just as enthusiastic about the success of others as you are about your own.

To forget the mistakes of the past and press on to the greater achievements of the future.

To wear a cheerful expression at all times and give a smile to every living creature you meet.

To give so much time to improving yourself that you have no time to criticize others.

To be too large for worry, too noble for anger, too strong for fear, and too happy to permit the presence of trouble.

To think well of yourself and to proclaim this fact to the world, not in loud word, but in great deeds.

To live in the faith that the whole world is on your side, so long as you are true to the best that is in you.

GRASPING THE GOLDEN RING

Quick Success Method: Love melts situations that seem impossible.
— CATHERINE PONDER

DURING DINNER ONE NIGHT, one of my new friends looked at me and asked the question I didn't want to hear –

"How did you become homeless?"

By now, most people have heard my story of being on the streets of Dallas in the late 1970s and struggling in poverty in Houston for many years after that.

But I had never explained exactly *how* I ended up in such dire circumstances. When I answered the question at dinner, everyone at the table stared at me. The woman who asked the question sat there with her mouth open and eyes un-blinking.

She asked, "Why have you never said this before?"

My friend Mark Ryan was sitting there, also staring, and said, "As long as I've known you, you've never told this story before. It's riveting. This changes everything."

Changes everything?

Riveting?

They all said I had to tell the story now.

"Given the current financial crisis and with people losing their homes and their jobs, this story needs to be told more than ever before," Mark said.

I heard them and realized I agreed.

So here's the story…

I knew I wanted to be an author when I was a teenager. I wanted to write books and plays that made people happy. Everywhere I looked I saw unhappy people. I believed I could help them with humor and stories.

During that time of the mid-1970s, I watched sports. I don't today but back then the Dallas Cowboys were the rage. Roger Staubach and Tom Landry were heroes. I got caught up in the excitement and felt the place for me to make my name was in Dallas, Texas.

I lived in Ohio at the time. Born and raised there. I worked on the railroad as a trackman, doing heavy labor all day long, working weekends and summers from the age of five.

I saved my money, packed up my bag, and took a bus to Dallas. It took three days to get there. I was lost in the big city, of course. Being raised in a small town in Ohio didn't prep me for the hustle and bustle of a city the size of Dallas.

Before long, I wanted out.

But I still wanted to be an author.

At that time major companies were building oil and gas pipelines in Alaska and the Middle East, and offering to pay big bucks if you were willing to go to either place. I wasn't keen on going to a foreign country and doing more labor, but I saw a chance to make money, save it, and then go on a sabbatical where I could write for a few months or even a year. It seemed like a brilliant strategy.

I answered one of the newspaper ads that promised to get me pipeline work at an extraordinary hourly wage. I went to their company's office, met an upbeat sales person, and ended up giving him all of my money – my entire savings, about $1,000 – based on his promise that I'd have overseas pipeline work in a week or two. You might guess part of what happened next – but you won't guess all of it.

Within a week or so, the company that took all of my money went out of business. Their doors were closed, no one answered the phone, and no forwarding addresses could be found. Shortly after that, the company went bankrupt. And not long after that, the owner of the company committed suicide. There was no one left to try to get my money back.

I was alone.

I was broke.

I was in Dallas, far from home.

I confess that my ego got in the way here. My family back in Ohio would have taken me back in and welcomed me back home. But I was head strong and determined to somehow survive.

Well, I did survive — by sleeping in church pews, on the steps of a post office, and in a bus station. It wasn't an easy time, as you can imagine, and I never used to talk about it. It was too embarrassing.

When I told this story at dinner, everyone agreed I had to share it with you. They said that people are finding themselves in the same situation — they trusted a government, or a corporation, or a person, or a bank, and now they are losing their homes and their jobs.

Hearing that I went through the same thing three decades ago and not only survived but prospered to a level that the Joe Vitale of 30 years ago could hardly imagine, ought to be inspiring to you, too.

I got off the streets and out of poverty by constantly working on myself — reading self-help books, taking action, scrambling at times by taking whatever work I could find, but always always *always* focusing on my vision: to one day be an author of books that helped people be happy and stay inspired. Along the way, I created the seven steps I'm going to reveal to you in this book.

If you're in a place right now that doesn't feel so good or seem too safe, I urge you to remind yourself that this is only temporary. As I say in my book, *The Attractor Factor*, this is simply current reality, and current reality can change. You can help it along by doing what you know and need to do. (You always know what you need to do. It's a matter of actually *doing* it.)

But remember, the sun will shine again.

It always does.

Your job right now is to focus on what you want and keep it in sight.

Yes, keep taking action;
yes, stay positive and surround yourself with positive people;
yes, be of support to others.

But remember, if I or anyone else can survive homelessness, poverty, job loss, or any other hard time, then *you* can survive it too.

Please hang in there.

One last thing:

I admit that there were times I wanted to throw in the towel and get myself out of this life. Thank God I stuck around. Had I left early, I would have missed a life of magic and wonder, success and fame I had never dreamed of before, priceless relationships and experiences, and much more.

I have no idea what wonderful good is headed your way — and neither do you. What you have to do is stay the course and follow your heart. I've written the seven steps in this book to help you attract money now. I know what it's like to struggle, and I know what it's like to succeed.

The latter is far better.

So let me tell you how to change your life...

I've traveled a great deal in the last couple of years – since the beginning of what's been called the worst recession since the Great Depression in the 1930s – and I speak to thousands of people about how to attract what they really want in life. Even those who were skeptical are now much more interested in finding out how to attract wealth. People are being laid off or losing their jobs, while their homes and assets have been slashed in value, and are now eager to hear what I have to say. Those that once found it easy to be positive and upbeat about their future are now frightened and unsure.

What's the solution to all this?

I've spent a great deal of time and developed many programs to help people find joy, happiness and financial freedom in their lives. However, many people have decided to sit on the sidelines until now. They felt their lives were fine, their relationships okay, and their career or business good. They didn't feel the need to try anything new or different. They were close-minded. Now it's a different world. The lives of literally millions of people have reached a critical juncture. They feel as if they're running out of options and searching for anything that will help – even if they used to think it was a little too far out of the ordinary for them.

Just writing that makes me smile because I was once one of the most skeptical, negative people around. I didn't have a dime to my name, a roof over my head and I'd borrow money from anyone and everyone that I could with no clue how I would pay it back. The interesting thing was that this happened in the 1970s and early 1980s as the oil market cratered and unemployment skyrocketed.

Sounds a little familiar, doesn't it?

I know what it's like to be unable to even imagine a future for yourself as everything that you thought you believed in crumbles around you. Back in those days, I would grit my teeth as the talking heads of the day discussed people's worries over how they would retire or when people's assets would recover their value. And here I was just hoping I could find some way to pay for food!

Each morning during that horrible time, I would see the same dejected, hopeless expression in my eyes in the mirror – the very same expression I see on many people today. Though I understand how they feel, and how you may be feeling about your financial situation, I know that with tremendous struggle and hardship comes tremendous opportunities.

What?!

Opportunity???

I know you've heard that before and might not have taken the idea seriously, but it's true. As humans, we tend to float along doing what's easiest or most familiar. We stay in our comfort zone. It may be lousy, but at least it's known. It's not until we are plunged into turmoil that we begin evaluating our lives and then, and only then, are our minds finally open to change.

I know this because that's what happened to me. If I hadn't been homeless and financially destitute, I might have trudged along living a boring, average life for the next few decades. But things were just awful. I couldn't keep going the same way. It wasn't working and it was obvious – even to someone as stubborn and hardheaded as I was at that time.

Financial hardship has a way of beating the pride out of you. Unfortunately, it also destroys your self-confidence and you become convinced you are hopeless. This is where the real problem lies. You no longer believe in anything. Not in yourself, not in your ability to overcome, not in the knowledge that tomorrow is another chance. You lose hope.

I can tell you from my own experience that this lack of belief isn't about reality – it's about perception. Just because you have less money in your pocket than the next person, doesn't make you less of a person – but it can make you *feel* that way. When everything around you seems to be faltering, it is hard to see the good. But that doesn't mean the good isn't there. Opportunities are all around you. It only takes one to change the course of your life completely.

Now, you may be thinking, "I couldn't attract money if you slathered me with honey and rolled me through a bank vault!" But that isn't reality. Anyone can attract wealth into their lives if they choose. It makes no difference what the economic conditions are or what the stock market is doing. In fact, the entire world could be in chaotic meltdown mode and you could still attract money!

Don't believe me?

THE PROOF OF HISTORY

You may have heard the saying that millionaires are made during economic downturns. Many millionaires were created during the

Great Depression. There is no question it was the worst time for many people, but did that mean all the opportunities dried up too? NO! In fact, thousands of people became millionaires. And back then a million dollars went much further than it does today.

Over the last 100 years people have proven repeatedly that attracting money has nothing to do with having the right education or knowing the right people. It has everything to do with your mind and your beliefs about money. I've said it many times but it bears repeating: if you aren't doing as well as you like, the only person standing in the way is the one you look at in the mirror every day. If you allow skepticism and negativity to dominate your thoughts it will soon devastate your bank account. Money will always match your mindset.

Remember that: **Money will always match your mindset**.

Contrary to popular belief, an economic downturn is a good time to start a business. Start-up costs are much lower in a recession than in boom periods. Savvy entrepreneurs think about what people will need as the economy improves and then position themselves to provide those goods or services. It is also true that many poorly run businesses close during a recession and their equipment and assets can be bought at fire-sale prices for pennies on the dollar. Commercial rents become inexpensive and there are many workers available as unemployment rises. This allows for many opportunities.

A good example of this is a man I met a few years ago named David. He was working construction doing small odd jobs around the neighborhood. After a few conversations I learned that he was actually a trained chef who'd been laid off a few years earlier from a local country club. He decided that the only way he would be truly happy was to open his own restaurant. His seemingly insurmountable challenge was that he couldn't afford the $200,000 it would take to open a new restaurant. His family was in the construction business, so he worked in it as well. This allowed him to earn a decent living and save for his dream – a "Jamaican inspired restaurant." I encouraged him to stay focused on his dream and opportunities would present themselves to make it happen.

A few months ago I ran into David again and asked how things were going. He was so excited he could hardly talk fast enough! One of the customers he's done some construction work for had some vacant commercial property in a prime location. It had recently been a restaurant that ultimately went under. All the equipment, dishes and fixtures had been abandoned in the building. The man told David that if he'd fix it up and reopen, he could have the first year's rent free and the next two years of rent at a substantial discount.

Needless to say, David's construction experience came in handy. He remodeled the interior and within two months, opened his dream restaurant, which made money from day one due to the low overhead. Would this opportunity have appeared in a boom economy? Probably not. It may not even have happened if David hadn't shared his dream with all his construction customers. David focused on that dream, and when the time was right everything came together to make his dream a success.

Just like business owners in the Depression era, those who open themselves to opportunity today are going to attract money! *Right now* while you're reading this. It's happening constantly and could be happening to you, but it will only happen if you don't let fear overwhelm you. Every time I see or hear something negative about the economy, I immediately think "Well, that doesn't apply to me." That's because I know how to attract money.

When I talk about past recessions and the opportunities they presented, someone will usually say, "But things are different now." My response is that they are and they aren't. Yes, we live in a different environment than past generations. Technology has made our lives easier and more complicated at the same time – and it has also brought us more opportunity. These days you can start a business from your computer, you don't physically have to go find a market or open a brick and mortar store as people in the past did.

One of my favorite stories is of Ashley Qualls – a self-made millionaire before she was out of her teens. Ashley, who was only 16 at the time, started a website called whateverlife.com from her home in Michigan. She wanted to help her friends get cool layouts for their MySpace pages and provide her friends with easy to understand HTML tutorials.

When she started her website, she gave all the designs for free. She earned her money from the advertising revenue. It was a very simple concept. Ashley saw the need and wanted kids her age to be able to get really nice page designs for free. The website now receives several times more traffic than most circulations of popular teen magazines including *Seventeen, Teen, Vogue*! - combined.

Back in 2006, someone tried to buy whateverlife.com from her for $1,500,000 and she turned down the offer. In September 2006,

Ashley attracted enough money to buy a home for $250,000 cash. She works out of her basement employing family and friends and is attracting money every day.

WE LOVE CHAOS

When I say that you can attract money into your life right now, I can't tell you the number of people who think that means they can sit on the couch sipping margaritas while money miraculously flies in their window and lands in their lap. This is *not* how it works.

In order to attract money into your life, you must follow the seven steps I have laid out in this book – and not one of them says to sit on the couch and wait. Attracting money requires action and focus; these can't be pushed aside or compromised. Unfortunately, humans are chaos magnets so unless we take the necessary steps to change our lives, we will attract obstacles and problems blocking our path to success.

I've also had people criticize me for presenting a program that focuses on attracting money. The truth is that most of my programs focus on attracting wealth as a whole. The difference between wealth and money is that wealth is what you have left when you don't have any money or your money has been taken.

Think about it. You may have a wealth of love, wealth in your spiritual life, or many other avenues that don't have anything to do with physical cash in the bank. Money, on the other hand, is your foundation for getting by in your daily life. It is your resource. Without money, or some sort of resource to survive, you can't focus on attaining wealth in any other area of your life.

But money is just a *first* step in achieving a better life, ultimately helping you to become more spiritual.

I can vouch for this personally. When you don't have work or know where your next meal is coming from, spiritual or emotional wealth is the furthest thing from your mind. Living today takes money and once you have that stable foundation it allows you to pursue those higher ideals. Money is needed and money is good. As you'll see in this book, money is also a powerful resource for doing good things for others. Money is not the be-all and end-all of your life. If you think it is, you are overlooking true wealth and giving too much power to money. Money is just a tool. A useful one, but just a tool nonetheless. We turn money into a problem out of habit and mindset.

Let me explain:

It is truly the human condition to find problems, create them, and/or attract them. Even when you resolve a problem, you almost instantly fill the gap with another one. We do this without even realizing it. You have to understand that as one problem disappears, another bubbles up to take its place. That's how the human mind works. Some people like drama and chaos more than others, but we all seem to attract problems simply out of human habit. It's our current nature. It's our program. And many of our problems revolve around money.

To paraphrase Buddha – life is suffering, but once you realize that life is suffering, you no longer have to suffer. You are free. At that point you realize that life is a theatrical experience and you are just playing your part in the script. You are detached. You are, in many respects, awakened. Yes, we are problem-making beings but you can also detach from the experience of the problems. You can witness them. You can watch them as if watching a soap opera on television.

I often see this in airports during delays. There's always someone who loses their mind and rants and raves. Will this make the plane take off faster? No. Will he get there before me? No. Does he love chaos and drama? Yes. I can sit and view the scene with detachment because I know that delays are part of the game. It is what it is – but many people haven't discovered that yet.

A problem to one person may be a blessing to another. It depends on your intention, which directs your perspective. So where is the real problem? Is there even a problem at all? Dr. Hew Len, my co-author of the book *Zero Limits*, often asks, "Have you ever noticed that whenever there is a problem, you are always there?" He means that the problem is yours — yours in perception and yours in responsibility. Clear the beliefs in you that see it as a problem and the problem disappears. Poof!

Your perception about money determines whether it is a gift or problem. The choice is in your mind.

I recently met a young couple, both surgical techs at a local hospital, that were facing a foreclosure on their home. The husband, Kenny, said he'd been in a state of depression for weeks and unable to see any options. I asked, "Options for what?"

He replied, "Options to keep our home."

"Why are you so convinced those are the only options?"

He stared at me for a while like I'd grown a horn on my forehead. But a home is just a thing – nothing more, nothing less. His emotional attachment to that home was altering his perspective. There are many options and opportunities that we encounter every day, but we are so sure that only one type of option or opportunity will work that we don't even consider any other possibilities. This doesn't mean it's easy. Kenny and his wife wanted a solution that included rescuing their home from foreclosure. I asked, "What would happen if you lost the home. Then what?"

He thought for a moment. "We'd have to start over."

"And what would that look like?"

Again he thought. "Well we could relocate to an area with higher pay as our hours have recently been cut at the hospital."

His wife chimed in, "We could even become traveling techs who earn even more money since we wouldn't have a house to hold us here."

As they talked, ideas flowed. Within an hour, they were convinced that losing this home was perhaps the best thing that could happen to them as it had prevented them from pursuing other opportunities that would have attracted much more money. They had been so caught up in the drama and chaos of the foreclosure that they hadn't looked at it objectively, in a detached manner. Once they removed all the negative emotions they attached to the event, they were able to think of many good things that would come from it.

When you face a problem or challenge in your life, it's only a problem because you aren't accepting what you have, and are focused on what you want with a feeling of lack or desperation. You need to be grateful for what you have now *and* want more. When you do that with awareness and detachment, the issue isn't really a problem, it's just your next activity. When you take the edge off your stress, you can more clearly see your next move.

Let me explain.

MONEY IS IN THE MIND

I've always known that the idea of money is in the mind. Most money is just a piece of paper or coin that only means something to the one giving and the one receiving. It is an agreed upon exchange of value. This is a very important idea to keep in mind. Often, when people think of attracting money, they think of cash they can take to the bank. While cash is included, it also includes things of value that come in from other sources.

For example, when David wanted to open his restaurant, the offer of a free year's rent is just as good as cash in the bank, because it was money he didn't have to spend. I'm always amazed at the gifts and other things that just seem to flow to me effortlessly. It's not always money. Sometimes it may be my expenses paid to visit exotic places like Peru – where I can stand on the ancient stone steps of Machu Picchu and have a great experience. Other times it might be a gift that arrives unexpectedly like a beautiful handmade leather bag I once received.

When you think of attracting money, think of attracting anything of value that will enhance your life. Not only do I experience this myself, I hear about these types of gifts all the time through my blog or through email, as others are learning to attract money for themselves. While you may think that we are on a currency system, many things can still be acquired through trade or agreement without any exchange of money at all. This opens new realms of possibilities.

The idea that money is in the mind highlights the fact that what you feel, think and know about money, determines your ability to attract it. Again, money matches your mindset. Many of us have had a tumultuous relationship with money over the years. Once I finally figured out that the issues I kept struggling with were my own creation (due to the beliefs and perceptions I had), then I finally opened the floodgates and let money pour into my life.

I'm often approached by individuals saying, "I don't want to know about that mumbo-jumbo Law of Attraction stuff, just tell me how to make money!"

How do you expect to attract money if you don't understand how to do it? Just like happiness, you can't pursue money. If you do, you will become a slave to the pursuit. The only way to experience true freedom, is to attract the money to you, allowing it to flow and circulate for the good of yourself and everyone else.

Those who are desperately seeking money, often run around in a frenzied state of panic, not understanding that this mindset slams the door on all the riches that would normally flow toward them. Panic attracts more panic. Worry attracts more worry. Desperation attracts more desperation. In this case, like attracts like!

STOP!

The first step is to stop all the activities you've been doing and evaluate yourself and your mindset. There is no way you can take focused action in the right direction if you're unaware of your limiting beliefs that may be getting in the way. Until you commit to work on yourself, and your attitude toward money, it will always elude you.

Attracting money is not about getting lucky. It is not about a once-in-a-lifetime opportunity. It's an understanding of how money works and what attracts money to you versus what repels it from you. I have lived the worst type of life and now enjoy the best. And the good life can be yours too. I'm not special or blessed in some way. There's nothing making it easier for me and harder for you. We're all on the same field. I'm just a few steps ahead, but not for long I hope.

In the next few chapters I will be revealing seven steps you can take to attract money with ease. Though I have taught thousands of people how to attract things into their lives, many still have a difficult time applying the concepts to their finances. They seem to apply the ideas to relationships, their spirituality and even their careers – but when it comes to money, they just don't attract it.

Throughout the text you will notice me saying, "Do this, not that," or "Choose A not B." This is because I want you to be rich!! I want you to close this book and understand the path you must take to attract money into your life – no questions or assumptions – just the facts.

If you're ready to learn my easy seven-step formula for attracting money now, please keep turning the page...

GRASPING THE GOLDEN RING
TRUTHS & TAKE-AWAYS

- Economic recessions and depressions have always produced enormous opportunities for people willing to ignore the negativity.
- People choose to live in financial chaos and they have no idea that they can choose a different path.
- Attracting money requires inspired action and total focus. These can't be pushed aside or compromised.
- A problem to one person may be a blessing to another. It depends on your intention – which directs your perspective.
- When you face a challenge in your life, it's only because you aren't accepting what you have and are focused on what you want, with a feeling of lack or even desperation.
- The idea that money is in the mind highlights the fact that what you feel, think and know about money determines your ability to attract it.
- Attracting money is not about getting lucky. It's not about the perfect once-in-a-lifetime opportunity. It's an understanding of how money works and what attracts money to you versus what repels it.
- You will attract money in alignment with your mindset.

ACTION STEPS

- Write down your beliefs about money.
- Ask yourself if those beliefs serve you or stop you in attracting money.
- What are five positive reasons for you to want to attract more money now?
- Write down a problem or current complaint you have.
- Write out a way to turn that problem or complaint into a product or service.

{STEP 1}
ALTER HOW YOU THINK

Wealth is the product of a man's capacity to think.
— AYN RAND

LIMITING BELIEFS ARE LIKE thieves in the night. And some of your beliefs are much more costly than others. The direction of your thoughts and the explanations you give yourself are extremely important in determining if you will attract or repel money. **The first step to attracting money is to understand and alter how you think.** In order to do this, you must address your underlying beliefs - and don't think for one second that you can just skip over this step and go on to the others. If you do, you absolutely will fail, so don't be tempted to treat this lightly. This first step is crucial to your success if you want to attract money.

People usually enter my Miracles Coaching™ program when everything they have tried has failed or has only been marginally successful. They say they have 'tried it all' – and they have, except for the first step! You must align your mind with where you want to go and who you want to be, way before you become it. In similar fashion, you must understand how money works and what it really means to you, before you will overcome anything. Otherwise you will end up sabotaging yourself repeatedly.

Have you ever felt like you were just within reach of something you wanted and then blew it at the last second? This happens frequently in sports. One team seems to have the victory in hand and then makes blunder after blunder, until it ends up losing.

Why does this happen?

Mindset.

If you don't have the mindset of a champion, you'll never be one. People often think that they will have a wealth mindset once they have made a lot of money. The opposite is true. You must have a wealth mindset *before* you achieve it, because if you don't, you'll find yourself frequently getting close, but never achieving your dream. Think wealthy now and you will begin to attract money now. Simple.

There are three core beliefs that have to be released if you want to attract money into your life. There's no way around them and no way to avoid doing your due diligence. You must get past them or they will always steal your potential.

Here they are:

I LOVE MYSELF

The most important core belief that must be expelled from your mind is "I don't love myself." This is the first thief. Now before you roll your eyes and wonder what in the world this has to do with making money, listen up. How you feel about yourself determines how much money (or anything else that is good) flows into your life.

Did you know that every single person who hasn't attracted what they want, has this limiting belief? They don't love themselves. Until they get rid of that belief, they're not going to attract money, they're not going to experience success and they're not going to have any of the things they want. They will wish or hope to attain their goals, they'll attempt them, but they will level off and be frustrated, wondering "Why is it going so well for everybody else but not for me?"

When I say that you must love yourself, it means that you must have a tremendous level of acceptance of all your good qualities and be working on the qualities you want to improve. This is not an idea where you ever achieve perfection. There will always be more to accomplish and new issues that must be dealt with. As you grow in knowledge and understanding, you will achieve your potential. You will always be working on yourself. That's how I, and everyone I socialize with, approach it. I don't have all the answers, but I'm actively looking for them. I'm also open to working on anything within me that might keep me from attracting what I want.

All of this is like peeling an onion. Every time you work through one layer, another appears. In your financial life, these layers and challenges have nothing to do with the external environment. It doesn't matter if there's a recession or not, who the President of the United States is, or how the stock market is doing. It's completely and totally internal – within you. This is one of the reasons why limiting beliefs are hard to change. They are invisible and incredibly destructive.

Step 1: Alter How You Think

You probably know people who are doing very well financially. If not, I'm sure you've read about some. They're likely doing *really* well, no matter what's going on in the country. If you look at the stories from the Great Depression or at other challenging times, you'll find many people who have prospered and thrived – many of whom are still around.

People like Colonel Sanders who created his namesake chicken recipe during the Depression, opened a restaurant, and now the company has locations around the globe. Companies like John Deere, which you might have expected to disappear during the Great Depression, came out of it stronger and is still going strong. These types of companies are all around us and serve as examples of what can be achieved. However, it begs the question, why did these companies survive when so many others didn't? It's because their mindset made them immune to the economic conditions. They believed they could weather the storm and did. They found out that negative news is like a disease and you can choose to allow yourself to be infected or not.

YOU DESERVE TO SUCCEED

The second of the thieves is "I don't deserve it." It's directly related to "I don't love myself." If you have an important goal, and you think it's worthy or valuable, such as, "I want a new job. I want a raise. I want more sales" - and you're not achieving it - you need to look deeper. The reason you aren't progressing is likely because you believe that you don't deserve it.

Now you may think this is irrational, but is it? Have you ever had a nice suit that you only wore on 'special' occasions? Or perhaps a special set of dishes that you only use on holidays? The motivation behind these actions is that you feel these objects are too 'good' for you to enjoy every day.

I once had a friend who owned a small ranch. One fall he bought a brand new customized truck and came by to show it to me. It was gorgeous. He was beaming with pride and you could detect a distinct difference in the way he walked – like he was 10-feet tall. The next week I saw him driving his old truck again and asked what happened. He said, "Oh I just take the new truck out for special occasions, it's way too nice to drive around the ranch." What he was in effect saying, was the thought of the new truck was above him. It couldn't be part of his daily life because he only felt he deserved to have it for special occasions. You see and hear this thief rear its head every day when people talk about how someone else is so much better than they are and how they can't possibly attract certain things because they are just not 'for' them.

This is a clear indication of where their focus is – which is not on achieving their dreams, but on why they can't or why someone else deserves it more. It shows they don't value themselves or their contribution to their own lives. If you don't love yourself, you will never believe that you deserve anything of value in your life. You will walk around with the idea that good things only come to others – but they are not meant for you.

Now you may even consciously force yourself to say "I **do** love myself. Look at what a nice person I am and look at all these nice things I'm doing." But if you're not seeing positive results, they are being blocked by a limiting belief deep within you. Your results are simply a mirrored reflection of what's inside you. The outer always reflects the inner. When you experience lack of achievement or when you get close to a goal only to choke at the last minute, you are struggling with beliefs that must be addressed.

I know literally thousands of people who use positive affirmations every day as a tool to change their beliefs. They can be very effective. The idea is that the more often you say it, the faster you will adopt it as a belief. Unfortunately these affirmations are no match for a limiting belief that may be lurking inside you. The positive ideas you are trying to adopt bounce off like a ping-pong ball hitting cement. The only way to change the situation is to acknowledge the underlying belief and deal with it first.

MONEY IS A TOOL FOR GOOD

There is one additional belief about money that belongs with the other two thieves. This biggest, baddest, boldest, most insidious belief about money has been around for literally thousands of years and is still here now – *Money is the root of all evil.*

Yikes!

With this belief, how could you possibly think you're going to attract money into your life, while being a good, spiritual, holy person? You may have some money temporarily. Just enough to survive on. But deep down your subconscious mind will repel money away from you, because you don't want to be associated with evil. This includes sabotaging your efforts at success.

Step 1: Alter How You Think

This one belief has kept generations on the verge of poverty since the beginning of time. What's worse is that it is not even true. Money is *not* the root of evil, especially *all* evil. Actually George Bernard Shaw said it best when he said, "It's the *lack* of money that is the root of all evil." There's a great deal of truth in that. The lack of money puts people in a desperate mindset, and that is the true evil. When in this mindset, they will do things they may have never contemplated otherwise and often those things are very destructive – to themselves and/or to others.

The belief that money is evil actually stems from a Biblical reference stating that "the *love* of money is the root of all kinds of evil." (Timothy 6:10) Love of money refers to someone who is chasing the dollar at the expense of all else in their life. This principle allows greed and selfishness to manifest in their lives. Chasing money indicates a competitive mindset that will do anything to have more money. It does *not* say that money in and of itself is evil, but that people who love money are prone to this trait. The Dickens character, Scrooge, is the perfect example of this mindset. He loved his cash money and only wanted more of it – to the exclusion of everything else in life.

Of course when you have a biblical reference with that much power, it's easy to understand how it can be distorted over time. As more and more people believe that money is evil, it can be hard to change the precept and realize the truth.

Remember in the last chapter when I said that money doesn't have emotions and only makes you more of what you are? Think about that. The richest people in the world, millionaires and even billionaires don't love money. NO. They don't. They love the *freedom* that money provides. Money is just a scorecard. Always remember that you can't really achieve great monetary success unless you follow your passion. The money is secondary. Money flows to the wealthy because they do not chase it just for the sake of having more. They desire freedom. They *don't* desire money. This is an important distinction!

When you understand that money is neutral and simply an agreed-upon exchange of value, you will attract money into your life right away. As long as you think that money is bad, evil, corrupt, or that evil people are rich and rich people are evil – you're not going to allow monetary wealth to enter your life. It will bounce off of you as if you're made of rubber and you'll never even notice it, except when you look in your checkbook. You will know that you don't have any money and wonder why.

I went to Ohio to visit my family a while back and I saw one of my brothers, the youngest in our family. He's got a nice family and a nice little piece of property. He's a mechanic, so he's making some decent money. He's working hard and living what most would consider a completely normal and average life. But he looks at my life and marvels at it. I know on some level he's really confused, since he doesn't understand how all this money was attracted by someone like me – a person he grew up with and views as normal and average.

He asked me at one point, "How did you do it?" To answer him, I basically laid out all the information I'm giving you now. I told him how money works, what holds us back, how I overcame my beliefs and how I help others do the same thing. He said "That's never going to work for me. I could never do that."

I was stunned. I wondered, "How can he even think that?" But in his mind, in his world, based on his past experience, he has no idea how to attract money into his life. He has convinced himself that he is a mechanic – and only a mechanic – and that's what he's going to be for the rest of his life. That means he will always make so much per hour, and that's good enough. When you look at it from his perspective, you can understand this limiting thought process. He's raising his family and has people he loves and takes care of. He's got his little piece of property and his vehicle. He's doing fine. It's good enough for him. But he doesn't see his own mental process, nor does he recognize how his limiting beliefs are keeping him from an even better life.

Then we started talking about my car collection – which amazed him. My brother asked me, "How come you don't have a Corvette?"

I replied, "I don't have one right now. It might be next on the list, you know. They come in time." This is not a limiting belief on my part, but my garage is only so big (although I'm building a bigger one as I write this). Still, there are only so many cars that will fit inside at any given moment!

He said, "I could never have a Corvette."

Again, I'm stunned. I'm asking myself, what goes on in his or anybody else's mind that sets such limitations?

My brother's mindset is just like most others. He works at a job for a certain amount of money. That's what he knows and that's what he sees as his future. He doesn't see the big picture or the possibilities. Even with me standing right in front of him as an example of what's possible, he still doesn't see it.

Step 1: Alter How You Think

While he's talking, I'm thinking to myself, *I could name three ways you can get a Corvette.* It really struck me in that moment how very different our thought processes are. My thought processes can come up with all kinds of options, all kinds of opportunities. I listen to most people, and in 20 minutes or so I'm thinking *There's an idea they're not even acting on. There's something they could draw out and turn into a product.* But they're not doing it. In fact, they're not even seeing it.

It still takes me by surprise sometimes that my own mindset has changed so much. Not that I'm saying I am the awakened one. I'm still working on myself all the time - every day - and I'm sharing what's working for me with you. It's just proof to me that if you do the work each day, you'll make progress without even realizing it.

Just as I'm astonished at how far I've come, there are also those times when it becomes obvious how far I still have to go. Recently, I had dinner with Kevin Trudeau, author of the "Natural Cures" book series. I was telling him how I have published over 30 books, several of which have become bestsellers. I felt really good telling him.

Then he told me how he sold *30 million* copies of one of his books. Suddenly I thought, "I haven't accomplished anything!" But my point is that he's thinking differently. He's thinking bigger than I have up to this point and that means I still have a ways to go. There will always be more to reach for and more to achieve. The process of changing your thoughts to accept each new level of achievement into your life is the real challenge.

THE GIFT OF RELEASE

The first question anyone asks when I talk about the three thieves is, "How can I change my beliefs and thoughts about money?"

The first step is to evaluate what you believe and why. Awareness is a must, as you must identify what's holding you back in order to deal with it. Once you've identified the ideas you want to change, then you must get clear of them and release their power over you. I've written many books and offered numerous techniques for clearing old beliefs and I'm always open to new or different techniques.

The basic premise of any clearing technique is that you first connect with that belief and become aware of the emotion you have attached to it. If you feel you aren't deserving, then the first thing to do is connect with that feeling. Do you feel sad, mad, or worthless? Now realize that this is just a perception on your part. You choose to feel the way you do and you can choose to release it. I often encounter this belief with people who've been treated badly or abused. They feel undeserving because they were told that as a child. But is it true? NO.

Getting past your old beliefs means exposing them to the light of day and examining what they are and if they're valid. Usually, 99.9% of the time they aren't. We carry around a whole slew of beliefs from childhood. If you were made fun of in second grade because you were afraid to speak in front of the class, it may have created a long lasting fear of public speaking. But where does that fear stem from? If you miss a word, is the audience going to jump on stage and devour you? NO. Your logical adult brain can figure this out, but you also have to release the emotional connection. This is the real challenge.

Think back to a specific incident and recall those emotions. Does your chest feel tight? Do you hold your breath or cringe with fear? These reactions are not in response to a real danger – they are the mind reliving an old incident that no longer can even affect you unless you hang on to that old emotion – that blocks your progress.

A lot of people think that positive affirmations will overcome limiting beliefs, but I disagree. If you don't directly address the issue and just use positive affirmations, you don't release the negative emotions that are blocking your progress. This is why if you just use affirmations, without dealing with the underlying issues, you will have limited success, because the limiting belief is still there.

There are many different variations of clearing techniques. Brad Yates and I have a whole audio program called "Money Beyond Belief." It's available at www.moneybeyondbelief.com. This series focuses entirely on eliminating money beliefs that are holding you back. You can do this on your own, for limiting beliefs such as, "I don't love myself." "I don't deserve money" and "Money is evil." None of these beliefs are true, so let them go.

I want you to be aware that all of the things preventing you from attracting money can be released right now. Your life can change in a nanosecond. I remember when I first started doing seminars, people would ask, "Can I really learn this in a weekend? Can I really change my life in a weekend?"

All I can tell them is my own experience. I've had moments in my life where I changed because of a story somebody told me over dinner. I've had moments in my life where I changed because of something I saw in a movie. I've had moments in my life where I've been in a seminar and somebody said one thing – just a phrase or explanation of

Step 1: Alter How You Think

a concept, and it might not have even come from the seminar leader – and something shifted in me and I awakened.

You can have an awakening at any point at any time, including right now as you're reading these words. I know many people whose lives have been changed by reading a book. For whatever reason, whether it was a new idea they'd never seen or an old idea they were finally ready to hear. The words awakened them and changed their life.

I wrote this book with the intent of helping you break through your financial barriers. Most people will change other aspects of their lives – but money is the hardest area for them to grasp. You shouldn't feel trapped into sitting on the sidelines while others attract the money that you could be sharing. And you don't have to.

But you must decide. Are you ready to look into those dark, long-held beliefs and banish them forever? Are you willing to do whatever is necessary rather than what's easy? Are you ready to say, "Hey money!! Here I am! I'm ready to receive!"? If you are, then you're ready to learn the rest of the steps that will get you there, but you must commit to doing them all. Each one in full. Then and only then will you open the floodgates to your new abundant future.

Remember, the first step is to alter how you think about money. When you realize that it is a neutral force for good, and you deserve it, then you can begin the process to attract money now.

But understanding and altering how you think is only step one.

Let's move on to step two.

STEP 1: ALTER HOW YOU THINK
TRUTHS & TAKE-AWAYS

- Limiting beliefs are like thieves in the nights. The first step to attracting money is to change your thoughts and address these underlying limiting beliefs.

- You must have a mindset of wealth *before* you will ever achieve it because if you don't, you'll find yourself frequently getting close, but never quite achieving your dream.

- All of this is like peeling an onion. Every time you work through one layer, another appears.

- If you don't love yourself, you won't believe that you deserve value in your life.

- Getting past your old beliefs means exposing them to the light of day and examining if and why they're valid - 99.9% of the time they aren't.

- All of the things preventing you from attracting money can be released right now.

Step 1: Alter How You Think

ACTION STEPS

- Reflect on the three key limiting beliefs and write down which ones might be true for you at the moment.
- Write down the opposite of the limiting beliefs and reflect on what it feels like to deserve and enjoy money.
- Consider other beliefs that may be limiting you from attracting money, and reflect on the opposite of those beliefs, so you know you deserve money now.

{STEP 2}
GIVE WITHOUT EXPECTATION

Your wealth is hiding under the very thing you are afraid to do.
— JOE VITALE

WHEN YOU TAKE an objective look at money and how it works, it can be really confusing. Those who have money seem to get more all the time – while those who don't have money, experience struggle constantly. It's as if there is some secret that the wealthy know that they aren't telling anyone. There is a secret but it's not how to accumulate money. In fact it's not even about money. The wealthy know that if you chase money, it will always elude you. They also know that money has to circulate, meaning you are a conduit for money, not a receptacle.

This is the secret that causes so much confusion. Most people assume they're supposed to be a receptacle for money. You attract money into your life and it sticks to you like glue. In reality, it flows through you. You are not a stopping point but a conductor. I liken it to traffic on a busy street.

Imagine that you are in control of all the traffic lights on a busy street. The cars flowing by are dollars. If you try to jump out in the middle of traffic and capture the dollars, you do nothing but cause chaos. Likewise, if you set all the traffic lights on "red" in an effort to keep as much money as possible, you completely stop the flow of traffic. It then takes much more time and energy to get traffic flowing again. Here again, gathering a few specific dollars is not nearly as powerful as controlling an entire stream of money. You can direct this stream at will – which allows you to have the kind of life you dream about.

Wealthy people understand the concept of directing a stream of money rather than hoarding it. They know that money in motion is a powerful tool, while money just sitting is doing nothing but

Step 2: Give Without Expectation

losing value. Unfortunately, most people who want to attract money into their lives merely sit back and wait to receive it. That's not how it works. You can't stand over home plate with a big catcher's mitt waiting for your fortune to come at you. If you do, your efforts will be met with limited success because you're standing in the way!

When I explain this idea, there is usually a room full of people nodding and agreeing as if they get it. But it can be a struggle to actually understand the idea on an everyday level. This is because we're conditioned by everyone we know and everything we've heard that the way to riches is to accumulate them. This is why we have retirement funds and save for a rainy day. These things are not necessarily bad, but the idea that this type of mindset is the way to true wealth is just plain wrong. Once you see the true power of directing revenue streams rather than hoarding your money, it becomes obvious that savings plans alone won't get you the life you really want.

I'm not saying to be financially irresponsible, but I'm telling you that unless you change your mindset and let go of the beliefs you currently have about money, you're doomed to struggle, no matter how much money you have.

We all know people who struggle to make ends meet each month. It doesn't matter if they make $50,000 per year or $200,000 per year. They have a mindset that focuses on what they lack, so rather than being a conduit for more money, they constantly try to chase money or try to make their money stretch.

I spent some time with a man I've been acquainted with off and on for years. He was a long-time real estate investor, and known to pinch pennies at every opportunity. His real estate investments always seemed to squeak by and not make the 'big' money he wanted. Just five minutes around this man and you could immediately see his "lack" mindset – he didn't tip, refused to drink anything but water when he went out for dinner, and drove all over town to save five cents on gasoline!

Needless to say, my ideas about attracting money fell on deaf ears. He was convinced that making money was hard. He told the story of how his parents had survived the Depression by barely scraping by. They considered giving money to others a sin. My nickname for him became Scrooge because he thought anyone who spent money was one brick shy of a full load. Needless to say, he thinks I'm crazy to this day. But my income has soared and his has remained about the same as it was 10 years ago, which means he's going backward, not forward.

He's so focused on every dollar that he can't step back and see the big picture. Therefore his money doesn't grow.

It's a common misconception that it takes a lot of money to get anywhere. That is simply not true. Even a small amount of money applied in just the right way can produce powerful results. Not too long ago, after one of our notorious Texas downpours, a friend of mine called and said part of his ceiling collapsed. He never even noticed a leak. But over time – drop by drop – water had worked its way through the roof and rotted out the ceiling. It only took one good rain shower to bring the whole thing tumbling down. When you think about a drop of water, it looks and feels harmless – but drops of water over time carved the Grand Canyon. Don't underestimate the power of a little bit of money applied in the right way as it can often exceed tremendous amounts of money squandered.

GET IN THE FLOW

So if money needs to circulate, how do you start? Before I answer that question, I'm going to say that you must decide to set aside all those old beliefs you have about money – or this idea will make you panic.

The secret to getting money to flow through your life and be attracted to you, is to GIVE IT AWAY. Read that again and again. Remember what I said about setting aside those old beliefs? I bet you instantly had them rear up at the idea of giving money away. How can giving away money attract more money? Seems a little backward doesn't it? It's not. When you hoard money, you're stopping the flow. **Giving without expectation of return from a specific source is the second step to attracting money into your life.**

I've spoken and written a great deal on the Law of Attraction. This law isn't new or different from anything that you learned as a child. Simply stated, "What you put out into the world comes back to you several times over." If what you put out is positive, you receive positive returns. If what you put out is negative, then you receive negative returns. It's that simple. When you were young, you were probably taught the ideas of 'give unto others' and 'it's better to give than receive' along with other similar truths. These ideas are simple statements of the Law of Attraction. If you give freely, without any expectation of return, you will receive back in kind many times over – not to mention the sheer joy that giving brings into your life.

Step 2: Give Without Expectation

Some people think giving has nothing to do with making money. I believe they are intertwined. The more you give, the more you receive – which allows you to give even more. You can give to those you love or to those who inspire you. You can give to your religious organization or charity. It doesn't matter to whom you give, as long as it's something you feel good about. In short, give money to whatever or whoever has made you feel uplifted, inspired, encouraged or happier.

TWO LEVELS OF GIVING

There are actually two levels of giving. The first is well known to most people. It is called *tithing*. At this level you're giving 10% or more of your gross income to the source of your spiritual and/or inspirational nourishment.

Now I'm sure you've heard that you're supposed to give 10%. I have to admit that years ago I really struggled with the idea. Partially because I usually heard it from someone with a vested interest in getting me to believe it! People like ministers, non-profit organizations, and charities. I thought they wanted me to give, so they can have their cut of my money.

Back when I was trying to get off the streets and get my life together, I'd go to church and listen to those who talked about giving as a path to receiving and prosperity. I thought it was a total scam! I would sit back and listen suspiciously, refusing to buy into what I thought they were selling. I refused to fall for it. But the truth is that as long as I didn't 'fall for it,' I didn't receive money. I was choking off the supply before it even got started.

Even if I pried a few bucks out of my wallet, I would wait impatiently to get those few dollars back in return. The problem was my mindset. I gave grudgingly; not freely and with joy. I gave expecting an immediate return and accounting of the dollars I felt I was 'owed' by my giving. It wasn't until I learned gratitude and the real joy of giving that I was able to step into the flow of receiving. It is this joy of giving without expectation that must be mastered before you can move on to the next level, which is *seeding*.

There's a wonderful book called *Seed Money In Action*, by John Speller. John talks about planting the seed of attraction. This seed is giving. And giving has the power to bring more riches into your life. That means giving more than the 10% that you've been tithing. In order to attract more money into your life, you *have* to give. This is a universal principle, if not a psychological principle. When you give, you open the door inside of you to receive. The more you give, the wider that door swings open. Giving comes back to you, but it only comes back through the same opening you made. So if you've only opened your door a little, then a little is all that can come back to you.

If you're sitting here wondering, "Where's the money?" Then the first question to ask is "Have I been giving money?" If so, "To whom?"

Did you give to your source of spiritual or inspirational nourishment? This is important because you also want to attract more spiritual and inspirational nourishment for your journey. That source can come from anybody. Perhaps it's a waitress working two jobs to go back to school or maybe it's a performer with awe-inspiring talent. It could be the cab driver offering an uplifting story, or a woman from church who always thinks of others. It can be anybody.

Sometimes people hear me talk about giving where you received inspiration, and they say they don't know where they received it. That always amazes me. Just stop, reflect, and be honest with yourself. Ask, *Who or what inspired me today?* Your inspiration could come from anyplace or anybody. Maybe it was a smile you received from a stranger. Maybe it was a fortune cookie. Maybe it was from a minister, politician (it could happen), family member or friend.

When you are on alert for receiving inspiration, you'll note it. When you do, reach into your pocket and give some money to that person, place or source.

OPENING THE DOOR

A few years ago I heard about a little boy named Kirk. Kirk had a pediatric stroke six weeks after birth. I didn't know such a thing existed. The stroke means that Kirk can't walk or talk. A mutual friend of mine, Kevin Hogan, told me about Kirk. Kevin was raising money to get Kirk some much-needed therapy. I told Kevin "No." I said, "I'm already giving." I drew the line and said, "I don't know this kid or his mom."

It wasn't but a few hours later when it was really gnawing at me and I said, "Okay, I'm going to do it." I sent $1,000 – and it felt great! A few months later, I thought, "I wonder what else little Kirk needs?" So I wrote Kirk's mom. Kirk's mom replied that he needed an exercise machine. Kirk would strap into the machine and therapists would be able to move his body in ways that retrain his mind and body to connect. The machine would allow his brain and his physical body to start working together again.

The machine cost $15,000. So I went to my blog and told my readers that I needed help raising money. I told the whole story, posted a photo of Kirk, as well as a photo of the machine. I had a PayPal merchant Account set up that went directly to Kirk's mom. In short order, a couple thousand dollars came in. I was disappointed. I thought, "Why aren't people giving?" And then I thought, "Why aren't *I* giving?" So I got out my checkbook and wrote a check for the entire $15,000. I sent it to Kirk's mom.

This money was going to a stranger I'd never met, for a machine I'd never seen. The act of writing that $15,000 check was one of the most exhilarating experiences of my life. It was absolutely exquisite! I can't tell you how good I felt to know that I was writing a check for $15,000. I was homeless, living in poverty at one point in my life. I was on unemployment until the government cut me off. I was suffering, struggling, going through terrible times. Now I could write a check for $15,000 to a complete stranger. I felt *fantastic*.

The power of this gift opened the giving door in my life even wider – allowing more than I could ever imagine to flow back in my direction. The same day I sent the $15,000 to Kirk's mom, I received a check out of the blue for $35,000. I didn't write the check to get money. I wasn't looking for the money. This wasn't money that was owed to me or that I was rattling the trees for saying, "When is the mail going to come and bring my check?" I wasn't looking for it, I wasn't thinking of any of that. I gave with complete detachment to somebody who was actually inspiring me.

Kirk inspires me. His pictures show him looking like a little Buddha. He has a great smile, bright eyes and a loving side of him that melts my heart. I look at the photos of him and get choked up. I look at those photos and something inside of me goes, "What the heck are we complaining about? There's no excuse." This little boy can't move his body and he's happy. That was worth $15,000 to me. And then I received $35,000 unexpectedly. Incredible!

I've learned that giving is incredibly powerful. I really want you to understand that you must give. But you must give where you receive spiritual nourishment. Don't give mindlessly or automatically. Check into your heart and do those things that nourish your soul. I had t-shirts made a long time ago that said, "Where did you receive the most joy today?" Wherever you received the most joy today – give there.

You can give in a lot of ways. What I'm describing is a spiritual principle of giving away 10% of your income – called *tithing*. This is the first step to attracting more money into your life. If you want to go further, then the next level is the *seed* money principle. This is where you give at least an additional 10% to wherever you're feeling inspired. This is on top of what you've already given.

When I was struggling and finding my own path, there were times I'd look in my pocket and there was $5. That's it! And I'd think, "Well, 10% of $5 is only 50 cents." It didn't really seem like it was even worth giving such a small amount. After all, what can 50 cents really do? But I was looking at it backward. I was focusing on what the 50 cents could buy rather than how wide those 50 cents could open the door for me to receive. It wasn't the amount of money, it was about the spirit of giving whatever I could.

Almost everybody gets to the point where they don't want to give. They want to hold on to their money or they think giving is a waste. It's easy to assume, "I will give when I have the money to give. I will give when I have a million dollars. Just get me to the million dollars and then I'll start giving." But it doesn't work that way. Just like you have to have the mindset of success before you become successful, you have to have the mindset of giving before you have a lot to give. This is because giving opens the door. And if you don't give what you have now, you won't receive more money to give later. As you keep on giving, you'll receive even more. You only have to follow the guideline – give 10% to where you receive spiritual nourishment and keep doing it.

In 1924, John D. Rockefeller wrote a letter to his son, explaining why he gave money away. He wrote, "...in the beginning of getting money, way back in my childhood, I began giving it away, and continued increasing the gifts as the income increased..." Notice that he didn't say he waited until he was wealthy to start giving money. He started the practice as a child and continued it throughout his lifetime. It is estimated that Rockefeller gave away over $550 million dollars.

Years ago I wrote a book on P.T. Barnum, the famous circus promoter. He was a big believer in 'profitable philanthropy.' He was convinced that giving leads to receiving. And he was right. He went on to become one of the world's richest men.

Step 2: Give Without Expectation

The idea of giving has become a hot corporate topic. Many companies are learning that business expansion is closely tied with their willingness to give back. This is opening the door to receiving on a global scale. And the most important type of giving is personal and individual.

BE THE ELEPHANT, NOT THE GNAT

From my perspective, the biggest mistake that people make is to give out their gifts with an eyedropper. They give far too little and miss out on the abundance they could be receiving. You have to give a significant percentage of what you have to be in the flow to receive.

It took me far too long to grasp this concept – and for years I gave as if it would physically pain me. I gave as little as I could. What I received in return was equally small and miserly. This was proof positive that it didn't work. Where was my abundance? I expected the universe to shove an elephant through the door when I'd only left an opening wide enough for a gnat! Naturally, what I got in return was in proportion to what I gave. I gave very little and received very little – but I still wanted that elephant!

Finally, I made up my mind to test the "giving" theory. For quite a while I'd been reading inspiring stories from Mike Dooley of www.tut.com. I really enjoyed these stories and received a tremendous amount of inspiration from them. I decided to give back to the source of my inspiration and send Mike some money. In the past, I might have sent $5.00 (gnat) but this time I sat down and wrote a check for $1000 (elephant)! It was the largest single contribution I had ever made in my life up to that point. It gave me that tingly nervous, excited feeling – just like you get right before you open presents on Christmas morning. The big difference was that instead of getting the gift, I was giving it.

Mike was stunned. He got my check in the mail and nearly drove off the road as he headed home. He couldn't believe it and called to thank me. I enjoyed his childlike excitement and exuberance. It made me *feel* like a million bucks. And that's real important. Because when you feel like a million bucks, as a result of an event you helped make happen, you attract more money to make it happen again.

I quickly realized that the sheer joy I experienced giving the money, far surpassed the excitement he had in getting it. It was an inner rush to help him. I still rejoice about sending him the money, and just thinking about it brings a smile to my face.

I gave with no expectation of gain and some wonderful things began to happen. I suddenly got a call from a person who wanted me to co-author his book – a job that ended up paying me many times what I had given away (elephant!). Shortly after, a publisher in Japan contacted me, wanting to buy the translation rights to my best-selling book, *Spiritual Marketing* (later expanded and renamed *The Attractor Factor*). They, too, offered me many times what I had given Mike as a gift (elephant number two!). I swung the door open and received many times more than I gave.

A true skeptic can argue that these events are unrelated. Maybe in the skeptic's mind, they aren't related. In mine, they definitely are. When I gave money to Mike, I sent a message to myself, and to the world, that I was successful and had stepped into the flow of abundance. I also set the Law of Attraction into motion. This attracted money to me from a variety of sources – far exceeding the amount of the actual gift.

Think of a person or organization that inspired you over the last week. Someone that made you feel good about yourself, your life, your dreams, or your goals. Give that person some money. Give them something from your heart. Don't be stingy. Come from abundance, not scarcity. Give without expecting anything in return. It sure enough will come from other avenues. As you do, you will see your own prosperity grow as your life becomes full of elephants and void of those pesky gnats!

Remember, the second step is to give money without expectation of return from a particular source. When you do so, you'll begin to Attract Money Now.

Now on to step three.

STEP 2: GIVE WITHOUT EXPECTATION
TRUTHS AND TAKE-AWAYS

- When you attract money into your life it should not be your goal to have it stick to you like glue. You're not a stopping point – you're a conductor.

- Rich people understand the concept of directing a stream of money rather than hoarding it.

- Even a small amount of money, applied in just the right way, can produce powerful results.

- If you give freely, without any expectation of return, you'll receive back in kind, many times over. Giving is the second step to attracting money into your life.

- It's important to have a "success" mindset, so you can become successful. You also have to have the "giving" mindset before you have a lot to give.

- The biggest mistake that people make is doling out their gifts with an eyedropper.

- Don't be stingy. Come from abundance, not scarcity. Give without expecting anything in return.

ACTION STEPS:

- Write down where you received inspiration today.
- Give money to those who gave you that inspiration.
- Expect money to come into your life, but don't expect it to come back to you from the same place you gave it.

{STEP 3}
PROSPEROUS SPENDING

*Whoever said money can't buy happiness
simply didn't know where to go shopping.*
— BO DEREK

MANY PEOPLE DISCUSS the scarcity mindset. It really became popular after Steven Covey published his book, *The 7 Habits of Highly Effective People*. Some people think a scarcity mindset is the awareness of what we don't have in our lives, like it's a static force: I don't have a nice car, I don't have a nice house, I don't have money. It sounds like a statement of fact. But it's only a litany of limiting beliefs.

A scarcity mindset is an active ongoing force in your life. When you focus on what you don't have, don't want, and don't take pleasure in – all you get is more lack in your life. This is the gap in understanding. In order to get to where you want to be financially, you must understand where you are. Shifting your focus to where you want to be, rather than focusing on what you don't have, shifts you out of the scarcity mindset into receiving mode.

Do you have friends or family members who constantly talk about every bad or negative thing that happens to them each day – right down to the most insignificant event you can imagine? I have. They talk about how bad their jobs are, how they can never get ahead, how the country is in a downward spiral, how the cost of gas, lemons, or anything else is running or ruining their life. They also make a point to tell you how no plan or program ever works for them and how they don't have time to even look at doing something different because it supposedly won't work anyway. I find these people frustrating. I try to help these people and they slam the door in my face.

Remember, your lack of money, love, health, wealth and happiness comes directly from your mindset.

Not too long ago, a friend told me the story about a girl named Alicia. She was in her late 30s and had never been married. Alicia desperately wanted to find a mate and have a family. She constantly bent all her friends' ears about how she couldn't seem to meet anyone or find the right person. Any advice they offered was pushed aside with a quick, "Tried it, didn't work."

Alicia worked in a large bank as the HR manager and was constantly meeting eligible men – but she didn't even glance at them. She was so focused on the supposed fact that she couldn't meet anyone, that she didn't allow herself to see the opportunities right in front of her. If she had shifted her mindset to "I'm going to meet a great person that I can share my life with," instead of on her loneliness and desperation, she could easily have been married and had a family. But these are the roadblocks we place for ourselves.

We develop our "financial" mindsets from those around us. If those around us are negative, then we grow up with a negative mindset around money. When you think back to your childhood, you probably didn't have a lot of money worries. Most of us had food, clothes, toys and the basic items we needed. At the same time, we also heard adults discussing money and their beliefs about their finances.

I don't know about you, but all I remember hearing from my parents were the negatives. Even when things were going well, my parents always argued about money. If we had it, someone was misspending it. If we didn't have it, then there was no way the bills were going to get paid. Of course a lot of what my parents believed about money came true as they were attracting what they were focusing on – lack. I remember the embarrassment of being told to only use two sheets of toilet paper because it was expensive!

Our normal life was one of lack. What was most astounding was that we still experienced lack even while my father was employed and we were living within our means.

People will often come to me confused, wondering how two households with similar incomes, can have vastly different experiences. One household never seems to have money, while the other goes on vacations, buys new things and seems much less stressed. Contrary to popular thought, there isn't a special kind of math going on here. It's simply a difference in how they think about money. Therefore, they get different results.

Your financial situation, good or bad, is a direct reflection of what's going on in your mind. It's not a situation created by outside influences, the economy, your parents or anyone else. You are responsible for your own thoughts. And those thoughts produce your results. It's easy to look at the result and think, "Well that's the problem." How many times have you looked at a pile of bills and thought, "I need more money. If I had money, these problems would disappear?"

This is a lie. Even if you doubled your income, you would still feel a sense of lack. And as a result, your bills would continue to eat up all your money. You would merely live at a higher level. That's how someone earning $250,000 per year can get overdrawn at the bank just as easily as someone earning $20,000 per year. This is also why some people win millions of dollars in the lotto, and are in debt a year later. Their mind couldn't handle the sudden wealth. They have not used the seven steps I'm teaching you. They are not comfortable with money.

SIMPLE IT'S NOT

It sounds so simple to convey the idea: change your mindset and you'll attract money. And we all know it's not quite that easy. When you are in the throes of financial ruin, trying to focus on anything but the wolf at the door, it can be hard to maintain your focus. Yes you need to change your inner thoughts and beliefs around money, but it's a process, not a quickie solution, though it *could* happen in an instant.

There's no denying that a lack of money is just the symptom of a bigger disease. And you can search for a cure and refuse to treat the symptoms. You must do both at the same time – deal with today's issues while doing the inner work to overcome your own roadblocks. The change has to be permanent to stop "lack" in your life.

You need to take positive steps and deal with the reality of your financial crisis. Take small steps to deal with your debt, while learning these new ideas and concepts that will prevent scarcity in the future. Face up to what you need to do and face it without fear. You must think and act positively to receive positive results.

This means being action-oriented. You can't just sit there thinking positive thoughts without DOING anything to turn around your finances. You must take immediate inspired action, and come up with a new plan and work it. This means that as your mindset shifts to goal setting and positive thoughts, you are seeking to dig yourself out of the pit. This isn't a magic formula; it's practical advice with no nonsense. Don't kid yourself into believing that you will be successful and attract money if you don't take care of the perceived mess you're in now.

It's been my experience that there are three different types of people when it comes to money. There is a small percentage of individuals on the verge of financial ruin, where desperation, panic and fear are real. I would call these people financially disempowered. They are faced with such difficult choices and realities that it may seem hopeless. I've been in their shoes before and can say that it is not hopeless – but it does require a significant commitment to improve your life. I was tempted to give up and quit many times. You have to make the decision never to give up. It's not an option.

The next group of people is the financially empowered. They attract money with seemingly little effort, and aren't bothered by external financial concerns. They will always be able to generate money.

Between the financially disempowered and empowered, there is a huge expanse of the population. These people are somewhere in between the two extremes and are the most susceptible to fear. They are the ones who are doing okay, or getting by – perhaps even living reasonably well - and they still worry that it all could crumble. They don't seem to have enough money to live the life they really want to live. Still, they see occasional glimpses of how great their life could be.

Interestingly enough, this last group is the one that struggles the most and lives with a mindset of scarcity. You would think that those near financial ruin would top the list, but when you are on the bottom, the only way you can go is up. This means you don't have as much fear of loss. It is this fear of loss that keeps people in jobs they hate or working for someone else rather than pursuing their own dream. The fear of losing what little they have constantly trumps the possibility of a better life.

You may be someone (or know someone) who constantly says, "I can't afford it." It doesn't matter what it is or what it costs; that's their mindset. A lot of it comes from the media. You may listen to the media – television, newspapers, online reports. This is a HUGE mistake. All they do is focus on bad news, which is not reality.

When I went to Kent State University in the 1970s, I studied to be a reporter. I took many journalism courses. Unfortunately, all they did was teach that good news is no news. When someone gets a new job or helps an old lady across the street, this isn't news. On the other hand, if there's a murder, theft, or swindling, that's news.

Step 3: Prosperous Spending

As far as the media is concerned, bad news sells – so that's what they focus on. Each and every time you watch the news you're giving yourself a huge dose of negative ideas. You are being programmed and your fear mindset is being created. There's war, famine, financial crisis – oh my, the sky is falling! Then you spend time around others who watch the same negativity and it creates a cycle of fear. That fear, real or media-induced, encourages you to be fearful and hoard your money in the face of crisis. This keeps untold millions of people trapped working hard for someone else and fearing that it will never be enough.

The good news is that this doesn't have to be you. Turn off the mainstream news, quit listening to the negative people in your life and keep reading this book. I'm about to tell you one of the greatest secrets to attract money now.

LEARNING TO SPEND

Money is just as much about spending as receiving. **Prosperous spending, or prosperous purchasing, is the third step to attracting money.** It's a phrase I coined to describe a step in the attract money now process that few know about. Yet it works like magic.

Remember that money must circulate. You spend money every day, but you have to ask yourself – do you spend it fearfully or joyfully? I'm not talking about going out and running up debt or spending money on a whim. Do you joyfully spend your money to enhance your life? If you have the money to buy something that will enhance your life and give you joy, you should do it.

One of the biggest paradigms that people carry over from their parents is the idea that spending on yourself is extravagant and they feel guilty about it. Recognize this mindset for what it is – scarcity. You live life once and if you never enjoy your days, fearful that you might need those extra dollars, then you will be disappointed at the end of your life. By little things I don't mean you have to go out and purchase a new car or home – unless this is your dream and you have the money to buy it.

Gerry, a millionaire, recently shared a story with me. He told me about the day that he finally understood the idea of prosperous spending. It happened in the grocery store. Gerry grew up without much money and his mother had always stretched the food budget. One day Gerry's wife asked him to stop and pick up a few things on the way home.

While shopping in the produce aisle, Gerry spotted some red bell peppers. He loved red bell peppers and put a couple in his cart. After a few minutes, he felt guilty, and turned around to put them back. At that moment it suddenly struck him that he was denying himself something he really enjoyed because of this belief he'd gotten from his mother – the belief that he needed to stretch the food budget. He was a millionaire who could've purchased a whole field full of red bell peppers! He said he bought eight and enjoyed every one.

We deny ourselves the smallest comfort or pleasure; even if it only costs a few dollars. This is not prosperous spending. Prosperity says you can have red bell peppers instead of green, rib eyes instead of sirloin, and romaine instead of iceberg. It's not about spending everything you make, but enjoying what you do spend, without feeling guilty about it. You want to feel good, positive and excited about your life even if you aren't where you want to be just yet. You still deserve to enjoy yourself and be happy. The positive feelings and emotions that prosperous spending brings is what attracts more positive things into your life.

When great things happen to me I like to reward myself. It is like saying "Job well done." It makes me feel great too. You should always reward yourself. When you reach a goal you've been striving for, purchase something nice for yourself or spend the day at the spa if that's what you like. Or take a weekend and go fishing at your favorite secret spot. Rewards don't have to involve large amounts of money – but they should generate large amounts of positive feelings and emotions.

A few years back I was speaking at a trade show. I had my own booth where I sold my books and programs. I was supposed to be there for four days. Each day after my sessions, people kept flooding my booth wanting to buy my materials. Within two days I was completely sold out. I was excited and happy that so many people got my message and understood what I was trying to convey. I decided to reward myself with a good cigar.

Now, I'm not a cigar aficionado by any stretch of the imagination, but I'm learning. I walked into a cigar shop looking for a reward and found some amazing lighters. I'm not an expert on lighters, either. Still, I wanted one. The lighter was a perfect reward because every time I'd open it, I would remember this day and my success at the trade show.

I didn't want a disposable or cheap metal lighter. I wanted one that said I'd done well and succeeded. So I asked the guy at the store,

Step 3: Prosperous Spending

"If Donald Trump walked in here, what kind of cigar lighter would you sell him? That's the one I want to see." So the guy walked over, unlocked a special case and pulled out a tray of gorgeous lighters. One really caught my eye. It was a dazzling gold Dupont lighter. It looked like success feels - bright, shiny and valuable. He took the lighter and opened the lid. I heard a 'ping' sound. He said, "That is the ping of status."

It was perfect!
But it cost $700.
Seven hundred dollars!
For a *lighter*?
I bought it and felt fantastic.

The next day I was telling some people about the lighter and there was one person who was absolutely disgusted. He said, "Why did you spend that kind of money on a lighter when you can get matches for free? Nobody needs a $700 lighter."

He's right. I don't need one, but "need" isn't the point. Another man who was there said, "I know exactly why you bought that lighter. You anchored in your success with emotion. You wanted to reward yourself for accomplishing your goal. You should have bought the lighter and felt great about it." And I did.

This doesn't mean you should go out and buy a $700 lighter. It means you should spend your money out of joy, not fear. You should reward yourself for meeting goals and making progress. You should generate as much positive emotion as possible with what you have.

The joy of spending your money is tied to giving – even to yourself. You are letting go of those emotions of guilt and fear, and giving yourself permission to enjoy your life as you also work to improve it.

But when you give or spend, there will be times when your old beliefs rear their ugly heads. You'll question what you're doing. You'll question me. That's normal. Change is a process, and once you accept that, you may even laugh at the silly things you do or say that have nothing to do with prosperity. And that's okay. In fact, it's a great way to take little setbacks and use them to move forward faster because it's positive emotional reinforcement. I've collected numerous little stories from people over the years regarding the moment they realize they were not in a prosperity mindset. See if a few of these sound familiar:

- I went to the movies, got popcorn, but left off the butter because it was an extra $.50. Two hours of dry popcorn to save $.50?
- Refused to pay $6 to wash my car. Did it myself and was sick for two days with sunburn.
- I built a house and decided to save some money on utilities by not living in it. Smart, huh? I spent the summer in a RV on the property with my husband, a five year old and two dogs. No amount of savings was worth that long miserable summer!
- My dad comes to visit and refuses to use the new towels in the guest bathroom. I got irritated with him until I realized I never use the 'good' towels either. So I threw out all the old ones and bought some fluffy new ones that were just for me. Who wants to dry off everyday with sandpaper?
- We used to go out to this fancy ocean side seafood restaurant once a month. The two of us loved the sea air and atmosphere but felt that it was too nice for more frequent visits. It's not that we couldn't afford it, we just didn't go and denied ourselves of something we loved.

We have all done things completely out of habit that seem almost ridiculous when viewed with a prosperity mindset. There will be many times when you may ask, "What was I thinking?" Truthfully, you weren't. You were on autopilot allowing all your accumulated beliefs to direct your actions. This is why it can be challenging to change those beliefs. They're deeply ingrained in your mindset and it takes awareness, attention and action to remove them. This awareness will allow you to catch yourself at times when you do or say something that reveals one of these limiting beliefs. A great way to become more aware is to listen and observe the actions of others.

Have you ever been in a mall for a few hours, listening to the people around you? The conversations and actions are revealing. I take a note pad and write down how many positive and negative statements I hear. I'm warning you now to make plenty of room on the negative side! The amount of negative statements will amaze you. People don't even realize how their words and phrases sound or how revealing they really are. I also make a column on my notepad called the "I can't afford it" column. I hear this one all the time.

Step 3: Prosperous Spending

As you learn more about circulating money, you'll eventually learn to balance receiving and spending so that both are positive influences in your life. They will keep the stream of cash flowing and increasing over time. Once you understand these concepts you can start investigating the ideas, products or businesses that will get you there. But until you do this work on yourself, you'll be marginally successful at best. When you have the positive prosperity mindset, then almost anything you decide to pursue will succeed.

The whole idea of attracting money is to enjoy your life. But you don't have to wait for money to start rolling in to feel joyful. Make the decision to pay attention to what you spend money on and the attitude you possess when doing so. Choose to add things to your life that give you good positive feelings, while you're working on your goals. When you attain your goals, reward yourself. You deserve it.

If you've been following my career, you know over the last few years I've been attracting a car collection. Not a collection on the scale of Jay Leno or Jerry Seinfeld, but good enough to get into magazines such as *Heavy Hitters* and *Austin Fit*, and on TV shows like Discovery Channel's upcoming new one on Super Cars.

The other thing you may or may not know is that I rarely go seeking these cars. They come to me. I'm just alert enough to seize the moment when the car is there. I say "Yes!" to them. And that is a secret to how the Law of Attraction works.

For example, I knew Patrick Dempsey (of TV's *Grey's Anatomy* and many movies, such as *Freedom Writers*) had a Panoz exotic sports car because I've been to the Panoz factory, met the Panoz family, and heard his story. I also own Francine, a 2005 Panoz Esperante GTLM, a fiery redhead of a car.

Dempsey's car was custom built for him in 2002, with every street-rocket perk you could install at the time. He's a race car fan and driver, and knows what he wants in a barely street-legal exotic car. Panoz listened and built what he wanted. The result is a one-of-a-kind car. It's a supercharged V8 with 420 HP. Like my own Francine, it's an Esperante GTLM. In fact, according to the Panoz Auto Development Company, it was the *first* Esperante ever built. It was named *Tallulah*, after Dempsey's daughter.

I remember thinking it would be cool to somehow buy his car one day. But I didn't worry about it. I mentally set my intention and let it go. I had no attachment to it at all. None.

Then one day I got my daily eBay alerts for the topics I'm interested in (such as Panoz, P.T. Barnum, Steve Reeves, Joe Vitale, John Scarne, Bugatti Veyron, etc). To my surprise, Patrick Dempsey's hand-made one-of-kind Panoz sports car was listed for sale. Please note that I did not go looking for that car. I let it come to me. But when it did, I took action and bid on it. I now own it.

The same thing happened when I stumbled across Steven Tyler's rare Panoz AIV Roadster. I'm of course aware of the Aerosmith singer, but never thought I'd actually find or buy his collectible car. Well, I did.

And almost the very same thing happened when I learned that the 1976 Jaguar XJS owned by famous bodybuilder and actor Steve Reeves (Hercules) was available. It wasn't listed on eBay, but I found it while browsing a website about Reeves. I couldn't believe it was for sale. I bought it for a fair price, invested a lot of money to repair and restore it, and now proudly own it.

But remember, this isn't about buying or collecting cars; it's about attracting what you want with intent, detachment, and action. In fact, the more detached you are, the better for attracting results.

For example, when I was in San Diego last September for my Miracles Weekend event, I went to a luxury car dealership to see a Bugatti Veyron, probably the fastest and most expensive car yet made. I loved the car but didn't want to spend over a million dollars for it.

While there, I saw a 2008 Rolls-Royce Phantom. I had no conscious intent to buy the Rolls, but did (and did on the day the stock market dropped the most number of points in recent history). As a result of spontaneously buying that car, with no need or attachment, I created a whole new business: the Rolls-Royce Phantom Mastermind. This is where two people pay me $5,000 each to have dinner with me and ride around in the car for an evening. Talk about feeling prosperous!

Again, attracting a new car isn't the goal but only the *demonstration* of how this process works. If you think this is about attracting cars or "stuff", then you've missed the point.

I could rationalize my car purchases as investments in a private collection (they are), or as rewards for milestones in my life (I just spoke to 15,000 people in Peru), or explain that I intend to turn Dempsey's car into a hydrogen-hybrid (by fitting it with Ronn Motors's H2GO system, like the one used in their amazing exotic sports car, the Scorpion).

Step 3: Prosperous Spending

But the larger lesson is that these cars illustrate how the Law of Attraction works. For you it may not be attracting cars but something completely different. Like money. Attract whatever you want. It doesn't matter. It shouldn't matter. I'm challenging you to make the LOA process *conscious* – and to enjoy the ride as you do.

Finally, I confess that I had doubts and second thoughts before actually placing the winning bid for Dempsey's car. That's the nature of our monkey mind. But then I remembered a key principle in my course, *The Secret to Attracting Money*. It's the principle I coined "Prosperous Purchasing."

Prosperous Purchasing means this: when the product or service is there, and your desire is there, and the money is there, then *buy*.

Why?

When you buy under those circumstances — please note I'm specifically *not* advising you to go into debt or spend recklessly — you send a psychological message of self-worth to yourself, and you join the abundant flow of the universe.

In short, spending under those conditions will *increase* your prosperity.

Because I now own Patrick Dempsey's sports car — due to the Law of Attraction, the Law of Right Action, and the Law of Prosperous Purchasing — I expect to achieve even greater wealth, success, and happiness. And that's yet another secret to attracting what you want: your expectations lead to your results. As the title of my most recent book says, *Expect Miracles*.

Before I end this chapter, I want to say something to all the ladies reading this book. For some reason you have a harder time buying things for yourself than men do. In general, you are likely mothering and nurturing to everyone but yourself. Always love, appreciate and mother yourself. While your natural inclination is to take care of others, you will be better at doing that if you also take care of yourself. In other words, mother yourself as well as those you love. When you go to buy a gift for a child, remember to also buy something for yourself. Again, just remember to take time to honor yourself.

Remember, the third step – "Prosperous Spending."
Now on to step four.

STEP 3: PROSPEROUS SPENDING TRUTHS & TAKE-AWAYS

- A scarcity mindset is an active ongoing force in your life. When you focus on what you don't have, don't want, and don't take pleasure in – all you get is more lack in your life.

- We develop our financial mindsets from those around us. If the people around us are negative, then we grow up with a negative mindset. This must be overcome before we can receive.

- Face up to what you need to do and face it without fear. You must think positively and act positively to receive positive results.

- Money is just as much about spending as receiving. Prosperous spending is the third step to attracting money.

- The positive feelings and emotions that prosperous spending brings are what attracts more positive things into your life.

- Let go of guilt and fear and give yourself permission to enjoy your life while improving it.

Step 3: Prosperous Spending

ACTION STEPS

- Write down three things you would love to buy right now.
- Pick one thing that you could buy without going into debt or tapping out a credit card.
- Buy it.

{STEP 4}
ASK FOR HELP

Affirm and yet affirm once more. Your persistent prayers will succeed.
— CHARLES FILLMORE

DONALD TRUMP ENCOURAGES YOU to "Think BIG." Everyone should. I know I do. So should you. I've had many dreams along my journey. During the early years I stood in the way of those dreams. It wasn't just my old beliefs that stood in my way – it was also my attitude. It was me against the world! I could do anything. I was Mister Macho.

Back when I was struggling in Houston, I became determined to be a published author. I could do it – I knew I could – and I could do it myself. I didn't need anyone's approval or help. I was the captain of my own ship – just the way I wanted it – just as I had learned from authors like Jack London and Ernest Hemingway. I thought of myself as the Lone Ranger. All I needed was a horse and a pair of six shooters, and I was good to go. But I didn't realize that this attitude was preventing me from achieving my goals.

Something eye-opening happened one day. I heard the term 'Lone Ranger Syndrome' at a networking seminar, presented by Donna Fisher and Sandy Vilas. They pointed out that I was just one person and if I continued with the attitude that I could do everything myself, then I wasn't going to accomplish much. I had always felt that asking for help was a sign of weakness. But Donna asked, "When somebody asks you for help, how do you feel?"

I admitted that I like being asked for help. I enjoy helping others. It makes me feel good and even honored, that they would think I could help them with their problems. When I didn't ask others for help, I was denying those feelings and preventing others the opportunity to feel good. From that day on, I started asking for help. **This is the**

Step 4: Ask For Help

fourth step to attracting money into your life: you must ask for help.

Ask anyone who is in a position to help you. When you think about asking for help to reach your goals, there are two levels to asking.

ASK AND YOU SHALL RECEIVE

The first level of asking is spiritual. In time, I got off the street and was no longer living in poverty. But I was still dealing with a mountain of bills. Your problems don't disappear instantly just because you decide to think differently. It takes work and patience. I was making progress. I was still struggling to keep my household afloat. Those were tough times and we've all been there.

I remember having a huge stack of bills sitting on my bedroom desk. I would lie in bed, see the bills and cringe. I had no way to pay them. I kept them stacked in the order they were due. Maybe you do this too. It makes you feel like you're doing something, even though you cannot pay them. I would lie in bed wondering, "What am I going to do?" I believed I had no options with nowhere to turn. So I did the only thing I could – I prayed.

I asked God for help. It makes no difference what your beliefs are – praying to a higher power helps tremendously. You can ask the Divine, God or Spirit for help. I told the Divine, "I can't do this. I can't pull it off. I don't see what I'm missing, I don't see the opportunities. I don't see where I'm going to earn, receive or attract any money. Please help me."

Asking for help accomplishes two things. First, it opens the pathway to receive. You're telling the universe that you're ready and open to new opportunities, as well as accepting help to meet your goals. Prior to praying, I wanted to do everything myself, so I wasn't open to receiving or identifying any possible opportunities. My mind and heart were closed.

Asking for help also allows you to release some of your stress. I know when I ask the Divine for help, it frees my mind to go on with what I need to do rather than obsessing or focusing on the same old problem. It lowered my stress. I know that once I started asking for help, I didn't spend nearly as many sleepless nights staring at that pile of bills. I could finally sleep because I believed that I was going to receive help – and I did.

The idea is to ask for help from a higher source. Then let go of your stress and have faith your prayer will be answered. Finally, take inspired action on the ideas you receive and the opportunities that come your way. Ask and act.

Decide how you want to approach the Divine. It's important that you make this connection and allow the Divine to help you. You must ask over and over in a way that's spiritually correct for you. This force can see the big picture – your ego can't. When I was struggling, my ego was standing in the way and I had to ask for help to move forward. Because my mind refused to see the path, I had no idea there were so many different ways I could attract money. I missed out. Now money flows to and through me from so many unexpected avenues that I can't even keep up with them all. I'm constantly surprised and thrilled when a new flow of money appears in my life. This is all due to the fact that I continue to ask.

I always make time to ask. It's easy to forget or let it go. I like to spend time in my hot tub each night. This is my gratitude time. It's when I communicate with the universe and say things like, "I'm working on this particular problem and I don't know how to resolve it."

I ask for help and guidance so I can get on the right path. This type of asking also comes with responsibility. When I am shown the way, I get on that path and take action. This was one of the holdups for me early in the game. I had my mind focused on the idea that I could only receive money from certain places. When other sources showed up, I was reluctant to act and missed out. I'm stubborn, but I learned that following my gut feelings or intuition is always the right move. If I get the feeling to call a particular person, buy a certain book, blog about an unusual subject, I do it right away, without questioning why.

MASTERMINDING TO SUCCESS

The second level is to ask other people for help. I'm not the best at this and don't always ask for help when I should. I will often wait until I'm backed into a corner and then ask. If I'd just asked in the first place, things would go much smoother. This is one of the reasons I founded the Joe Vitale's Miracles Coaching™ program and the Hypnotic Marketing Coaching program. All of us need help. Everyone from the person struggling to get off the streets to the top CEOs running billion dollar companies, needs good advice and needs help.

When you receive help from another person, you both benefit from the positive flow of energy and the combined force of your wills. When you have at least two people or more who get together to discuss

Step 4: Ask For Help

an issue or possible options, you get a wonderful mixture of ideas and encouragement. Far more than you would ever expect. This is because each of us has limitations. As a group we ask each other, as well as the Divine for help. This produces much more energy than you could ever generate by yourself.

I strongly encourage everyone to be in a mastermind group. This is a group of people, acting as a support team, who are like-minded and willing to help each other. Ideally the group will have six or fewer people in order to be most effective. Each person talks about their goals and the issues they've encountered. The ideas and options flow from all of the group members.

Mastermind groups are nothing new and have been popular since Napoleon Hill defined them in the book, *Think and Grow Rich*. These groups were key to some of the world's most successful business people and they still are today. Bill Hibbler and I wrote a whole book about "Masterminding" called *Meet and Grow Rich*. The idea of this type of group can be seen everywhere, from the presidential cabinet to corporate boards of directors. These groups come together to offer ideas to each other for running complex businesses or even nations. Every one of us can benefit from this type of support group.

I find it valuable to talk to people with similar experiences. If you've decided to start a business, it's wonderful to talk to experienced people. Learning about their successes and failures can shorten your learning curve and prevent you from making costly mistakes.

Having several people with varied backgrounds in your mastermind group is important because they have differing perspectives and viewpoints. They'll also be able to help you see things from new angles and understand certain issues that you may not have thought of yet. They can enhance your goals and objectives by bringing additional connections and resources to you that'll expand your business.

Let's say you want to generate media attention for your new business. One of the people in your group may have experience or contacts in the media that will provide an 'in.' This will help you get the coverage you want. It always amazes me how small the world really is. There have been many times while I've been attending mastermind meetings and a great idea would come up. And sure enough, someone in the group knew someone who knew someone who could help make it happen.

One of the benefits is the accountability and inspiration you'll receive. If I'm in a mastermind group and tell people that one of my goals is to have my own infomercial, I know that they're going to ask about my progress. This will motivate me to take action and get things moving.

For example, years ago I went into my mastermind group at the time and announced, "I intend to be in a movie." I had no acting experience nor any contacts. My group could have laughed and ridiculed my wild notion. Instead, they supported me. They simply held the same intention as me: for me to be in a movie. As a result, six months later I was asked to be in the movie, *The Secret*. The rest, as they say, is history.

I'm not saying you'll end up in a movie by being in a mastermind (you might). I am saying they are powerful tools for helping you attract money and achieve goals.

Creating this type of group is easy. In fact you may already have a loose association of people that would be interested in forming this type of group. Treat each member like they're part of your own board of directors. You don't want just anyone in your group. You want those people who have backgrounds that match what you're working on. For example, if you want to own a restaurant, your group may be made up of another restaurant owner, accountant, banker, lawyer, insurance agent or even a food wholesaler. These contacts can offer a wide range of advice and help that will prove extremely valuable to you.

One word of caution: do not automatically include your friends and family unless they're going into business with you. Even then you must be cautious. It's a natural tendency to include those you love, but you must realize that they'll be operating from their own belief systems – many of the same beliefs you are trying to move past. My family is still shocked that I've done so well. It seems to confuse them as they only see me as their brother, uncle, or son, rather than as a marketer or businessman. While family and friends usually mean well, it's rare they would have the skills needed to push you along in your quest for success.

To create a mastermind group dedicated to your success, you need to reach out to your current network. Remember that everyone knows someone who knows the right person. So let them know that you are asking for their help as an advisor and part of your mastermind team. You will be surprised at how willing people are to help when asked. They feel honored. And you're offering them the opportunity to participate in something that makes them feel good. They are helping themselves while they are helping you.

Step 4: Ask For Help

They may participate by phone or in an informal setting. They may be all together or one-on-one. Do whatever works for you. You can even set up discussions by email so everyone stays in the loop. With modern technology it's much easier to reach out to those who aren't even in your geographical area. Some of my best advisors are international and we can easily communicate from anywhere around the world.

If you want to be in an online mastermind, you may consider joining the Attract Miracles community at www.attractmiracles.com.

THE KINDNESS OF STRANGERS

You will find that people will come and go, while others touch your life each day. Everyone has something to offer. I've stayed in touch with people through my blog. I get tons of support and encouragement through this one channel alone. I'm able to help people like little Kirk, as well as others. I receive money, gifts and great opportunities because I'm willing to put myself out there and let people get to know me.

I have to admit it was a little strange having people I did not know come up and talk to me as if they knew me. They got to know me from reading my blog. It was hard for me to get used to, but before long, I recognized the power that this offered.

It's been difficult for me in the past to open up to anyone. This is why I still sometimes find it hard to ask for help. I know many other people struggle with this same issue. What I've gained by allowing people into my life has far outweighed any uncertainty or reservations I once had. Having said that, I still try hard to remember that there are specific actions I can take to enhance all my relationships.

The easiest part is to find out how I can help them. People fascinate me. I'm curious as to how they think and what makes them tick. Just like the conversation I had with my brother, when I encounter a new person, I want to know what their goals are, what they dream about and how I can help. Now they can either take my advice or not, but I'm there to help – which opens me to receive help from them as well. It is a constant flow back and forth.

This type of give-and-take means you must have a generous heart. You must be willing to give yourself and your ideas to others. I have known many people who refused to offer ideas because they were afraid their ideas would be "stolen." I can tell you that there are no new ideas. The universe will give someone else the same idea if you don't act on it. I can also say from experience that when you help someone succeed, they'll go way out of their way to help you in return. This has happened repeatedly to me.

One of the mistakes I made was to let people flow in and out of my life without following up or making a real connection. I didn't follow up or stay in touch. I can say that it's very easy to do, especially when you start doing well. You get busy. And if you don't take time to make contact with people, you'll lose some of your momentum. I always remember that each person I encounter may be the catalyst for my next big success, and to overlook that or cast it aside, is to waste their gift.

I provide value to others. But does that mean I am always right? NO. I'm human. And when I make a mistake or mess up, I'm usually the first one to admit it. You don't have to pretend to know it all or pretend that everything is fine or that you don't need help. We all need help. And by allowing people to know your vulnerabilities, it attracts knowledge and resources to you that you may not have had otherwise. I went for years thinking I had to be a mysterious, struggling writer, trying to make a living. I kept to myself and didn't let people know my real situation. Now I'm convinced that it prolonged my agony for no reason. Be authentic and people will respond to you.

No matter what level of success you achieve, you will not do it by yourself. I constantly remind myself to be grateful for every single person who helps me. I say thank you at least once a day. I know I'm just one person and without others, I would still be in a dark little room in Texas banging out my next book on an antiquated computer. I have seen some business people who barely even noticed those around them who made things happen. They treated their assistants and coworkers like dirt! I can't imagine ever working for someone like that. I'm sure every person who is treated in such a bad manner only does the minimum required when their full effort could be such a huge benefit. I don't want to be one of those people. By expressing my gratitude everyday, I stay grounded and am reminded that I'm just a guy with a dream. If it wasn't for the kindness of others I'd be in big trouble.

It takes a big person to give credit to others, but the positive emotion it brings is tremendous. I don't mean that you should offer false compliments or platitudes – just point out what people do well. There's a special feeling you get when someone comes to you and says, "I heard such great things about you from someone you worked with last year. I want to pursue the possibility of working with you as well." That kind of comment can make my day! No one has to say nice things about you – especially when you are out of earshot. And when you hear something positive like this from a third party, it makes you feel 10 feet tall. Everyone you work with deserves the same feeling.

I find it easy to connect with people. This is even easier when you learn to laugh. Believe it or not, I used to be a very serious person. You'd rarely see a smile on my face and every time I looked in the mirror I saw a furrowed brow. I thought that life was this serious life-and-death struggle and that I had to stay on my toes or it would bury me. Life comes at you whether you're ready or not. And if you can meet your challenges with a smile on your face and laughter in your heart, then you are the kind of person that others want to be around. You don't have to treat every decision as if your whole existence is riding on it. Not only will you benefit from a relaxed state of mind – but so will everyone around you.

As you focus on helping everyone you come into contact with, you will soon be reaping the benefits. Their knowledge and experience will lift you to a new level. The important lesson is to freely give to others without the expectation of getting anything in return from them. The receiving will come naturally with these relationships just as it does when you give money. Investing your time and emotion in others is a great investment. This will get you through difficult times while keeping you motivated and inspired.

I've read dozens of financial books and they always start out with do A, then do B, then do C and all will be right. That's crazy. It doesn't start with doing – it starts with being. You must get your thoughts and beliefs in line. Then you must get help. If you think you can do this by yourself, you're setting yourself up to be disappointed.

I have given many talks about money in the past few years, all over the world, and the participants always start with "How? How do I get the money?" You need to understand that it has nothing to do with dollars and cents and everything to do with just getting into the flow. That won't happen if you run around chasing a dollar. Until you really understand and get that fact, you will never attract money.

There are many people who might try to tell you how to attract more money who haven't been where you are, but I've been at the bottom. I wasn't born into money and I didn't win the lottery. In fact for a large portion of my life, I did everything wrong trying to chase money and it didn't work. So don't think I'm telling you things that I haven't tried. I know for a fact what I'm telling you works, because

I've made every mistake along the path that could be made. When I finally understood these principles, I was able to overcome and so will you. All I can say is that if you already had the answer, you'd be a millionaire right now. So why not try something different that might get you there? You can't be any worse off for trying. What if it actually works for you, just like it did for me?

Remember, the fourth step is to ask for help: from your connection to a higher power to the people you feel can help you move ahead.

And now on to the next step.

STEP 4: ASK FOR HELP
TRUTHS & TAKE-AWAYS

- Asking for help is the fourth step for attracting money into your life.
- The first level is asking the Divine for help.
- The second level of asking is getting help from others.
- Asking opens the pathway to receive and releases the stress and pressure.
- When you are given a path, you need to get on it and take inspired action right away.
- A mastermind group is a like-minded support team whose purpose is to help the members of the team.

ACTION STEPS

- Pray in whatever way is comfortable for relief from your money concerns.
- Make a list of people who could help you attract money now.
- Contact each person with a respectful request.
- Contact five people about creating a mastermind group.

{STEP 5}
NEVILLIZE YOUR GOALS

*You have brains in your head, you have feet in your shoes,
you can steer yourself in any direction you choose.*
— DR. SEUSS

In order to get where you want to go in life, you must be able to visualize the results. In several of my books, particularly *The Attractor Factor*, I write about the concept, "Nevillizing" your goals. It's a word my friend David Garfinkel coined to explain an amazing process for attracting whatever you want – even money.

"Neville" refers to Neville Goddard, a famous mystical writer. I've collected his books and even have autographed editions signed with his message, which is, "Assumption hardens into fact."

He believed that if you're trying to attract money or anything else in your life, you don't just say, "I want money. I'm going to attract money. I now have money." You don't say any of those affirmations. What you do is go to the end result and imagine what it would be like to have those things in your life right now. **The process of 'Nevillizing' is the fifth step to attracting money into your life.**

Let me explain this to you.

It's important to focus and get emotionally involved with your goals. Let's say that you want to attract $250,000 in the next 12 months. This is a big goal for many people. When you sit and imagine what your life will be like, focus on the details. What bills will you get to pay? Think about sitting at your desk or kitchen table and physically writing the checks to pay them off. How does it feel? Put a stamp on the envelope and pop it in the mailbox. Are you smiling? Feeling proud of your accomplishment? Let those feelings and emotions consume you.

Now imagine what will change in your life. Would you live in a different home? If so, spend some time thinking about what it would be like to drive up to that house and know that you live there. Would you take an exotic vacation to the Caribbean? If so, imagine all the places you would visit. Imagine the beautiful ocean waves and the sand through your toes. What does it feel like to gaze across the beautiful shore and know that your success gives you the freedom to be here? This type of emotional connection to getting what you want is what I mean when I say to "Nevillize" your goal.

Use this technique for every single goal you want to accomplish. Now you may be wondering about all those people who tell you to do positive affirmations. These affirmations do put you in a positive frame of mind. But when it comes to actually achieving your goals, you will have much more success if you make that emotional connection in your mind, where you can feel, hear and experience what it will be like to actually have what you are striving for. Positive affirmations can keep you focused and on track. And once you experience something in your mind, you have created a big shift in belief. But saying something doesn't necessarily change your underlying beliefs, but *experiencing* it – even if it is only in your mind – allows your subconscious mind to believe it is possible.

Did you know that your subconscious mind can't tell what's real from what's imagined? If you don't believe me, watch a really scary movie! You body will respond to the idea of physical danger and send adrenaline flowing through your body. This will make your blood pressure rise and your heart pound. Your subconscious mind prepares you for a flight or fight response, even though your conscious mind knows it's just a movie. Well it's obvious that if the subconscious mind responds this way to fear, it will also respond in the same manner to good events – such as you attracting $250,000 this year. If you create that emotional connection, the mind reacts as if it's real. If your mind can scare you out of your wits at a movie, it also can convince you that you will attract $250,000 this year.

PUT IT INTO PRACTICE

You may be just like I used to be. You won't believe it until you test it out. So, test it. Imagine that you will attract a specific amount of money over the next 30 days. It may be $1000, $2000, $5000 – whatever you feel is reasonable for you. You don't know where it will come from, but you know it's coming.

You must be very clear that it will happen and that it will be a specific amount. Now close your eyes and imagine opening your

Step 5: Nevillize Your Goals

mail and finding a check for exactly the amount you want. Feel that excitement, amazement and joy? Imagine running into your house and telling your spouse, children, and friends how you attracted the money.

One of my Texas seminar attendees was intrigued by this idea, but skeptical. Who wouldn't be? She understood the concept, but wasn't sure it would work for her. So I asked what amount she'd like to receive in the next 30 days. She wanted to do some small home repairs and paint one of the rooms in her house, and it was going to cost $750. So we sat with our eyes closed, and went through a vision of what the room would look like completed, as well as how she would show it off to friends. We also visualized how fantastic she would feel as she attracted the money seemingly out of thin air. She went on her way and about four weeks later I received an email.

Two weeks after the seminar, out of nowhere, she received a $602 refund from her insurance company. A couple weeks later, she received a $150 rebate on a television she'd bought the previous Christmas – more than 10 months earlier. This totaled $752 in just 30 days. Some would say that these things would have happened anyway, but would they? When was the last time you got a refund out of the blue on your insurance? And that rebate should have been paid months earlier – why now? There's a simple reason for all this – she learned how to attract it.

Keep in mind that it's your responsibility to act when a source of money is attracted to you. It doesn't always arrive as a check – it may be something that you can sell, or an opportunity to earn something additional.

I received a letter from a gentleman who wanted to find a way to earn $1000 prior to the Christmas holidays. He was on a fixed income and wanted to visit his grandchildren. He used this technique to Nevillize his goal of $1000. Not long after, a neighbor lady was helping him clean out a spare bedroom when they ran across a flute that his daughter had played in school more than 40 years earlier. The daughter didn't want it back, but offered to put it on eBay for him and see what he could get. It turns out the flute was solid silver and brought in more than $732.

A few weeks later, an administrator at the local community college (who knew this man was an avid hobby photographer) called and asked if he would be interested in teaching a leisure studies course on photography for seniors. He immediately said yes and learned that it paid $325 for the semester. Because he was open to new opportunities, he received more than his $1,000 from selling the flute and teaching a class. So don't have preconceived notions about how the money will arrive or you will cut off the flow before it even starts flowing. Just be open to receive it and you will attract it.

EXPAND YOUR VISION

Once you understand how powerful this technique is, you'll naturally begin to expand it to every area in your life. If you want to create a new and exciting business, then visualize your new office space, think about how your bank balance will grow, and imagine your day speaking to clients, customers and employees who are helping you to achieve your dreams. How will it feel to sit in your office and see what you've created? Allow those feelings to flow through you. You feel pride, gratitude and the sweet taste of success.

Many people marvel at how this works. In reality, it's not hard to understand. You are telling your mind to pay attention to the avenues and opportunities that will help you meet these goals. Does this mean these opportunities don't exist? No. It just means your mind filters them out because you haven't told it that these opportunities are important. Remember when we discussed the fact that the minute you buy a certain color car, it seems like everyone else has that same color? Once you buy a certain color car, your mind moves that color car up the 'important' list and you suddenly notice them everywhere, all around you.

This is exactly how the mind works when you're attracting opportunities. You're telling yourself that these opportunities are important so it should sit up and take notice. That's how it worked for the man who sold the flute. That instrument had sat in his closet for 40 years.

This is what happens when you start thinking about those opportunities. If you set your goal at $250,000, or whatever amount, and have no clue how it will happen, then you must allow your mind to help you work on it.

I frequently speak to people who are convinced that all the good opportunities are taken. When I tell them that there is no end to the creative possibilities, I usually get a blank stare.

I like to spend some time everyday reading inspirational, personal and business stories. Not only do these increase the positive feelings

Step 5: Nevillize Your Goals

that help me attract more money into my life – they also get the creative juices flowing for the possibilities.

I have always liked the story of Starbucks. If you'd have told me back in the 1970s that one day, a $4 cup of coffee would be the cultural norm, I would have told you that you were crazy! Of course I would have said the same thing about cell phones – but that's another story.

Howard Schultz is the man responsible for making the $4 cup of coffee a way of life. He was originally a coffee maker salesman and one of his best customers was Starbucks and Co. in Seattle. At that time the company sold coffeemakers, beans and other items, but did not sell cups of coffee in their stores. He fell in love with Starbuck's way of doing business and had a vision that premium coffee by the cup was the wave of the future. He wanted to work for Starbucks and they said no. But Howard held onto his vision and pestered them for a full year until they finally agreed to hire him as their director of marketing in 1982. One quote that I love from Schultz is, "Life is a series of near misses. But a lot of what we ascribe to luck is not luck at all. It's seizing the day and accepting responsibility for our future."

Schultz had a vision of people sitting in a coffee shop sipping fabulous brews and enjoying life, just as he'd seen on a trip to Italy. The company resisted his idea and soon he quit to start his own coffee shop. It was wildly successful and in 1982 he bought the original Starbucks for $3.8 million. Today, Starbucks is a multi-billion-dollar business. And it's all because Howard Schultz visualized this idea of a little neighborhood coffee shop where people could enjoy great coffee. It was a really simple idea when you think about it. He persisted and focused on his dream. When obstacles appeared, new doors opened to get around them.

YOUR ACTION PLAN

The first step in Nevillizing your goal is to ask yourself what you want. This sounds easy, but isn't for many people. What you want may change as you go along. But for now, decide what the overall plan is. Now I've met many people. Some were highly educated and, having completed their schooling, and started their careers. Most found themselves in a career they hate! It happens, but you have to be willing to let go of what others expect of you, or the guilt of considering how much time you've spent on your current path, and ask, "What do I really want?"

Some people immediately know what they would like to have in their lives and they can instantly start to Nevillize that idea. But what if you ask yourself what you really want and get a big fat blank?

I recently heard about a young mom from North Carolina, named Karen. She was in this predicament. She was married with a young daughter. Though she'd been trained in criminal justice, she quickly found the prisons and courts to be very negative and depressing places to work. When her daughter was born she had the opportunity to stay home and be a full-time mom. At that point, she decided to figure out what she really wanted to do with her life. She'd worked as a temp in many jobs, including one doing background checks. She knew she liked office jobs, but wanted the flexibility of staying home and raising her daughter. She just couldn't find anything she really wanted to do.

One day while watching an afternoon talk show, Karen saw a couple whose nanny abused their child. It turned out the nanny had a long criminal record. Karen was appalled as her daughter was about the same age and she couldn't imagine hiring someone to watch her child without doing a full background check. This sparked an inspiration. Karen wanted to save other parents' children from the same fate these people had suffered. And she wanted to do it from her basement. The next day she got her hometown paper and looked at the ads placed by parents seeking nannies and babysitters. She called them and offered her services. Several of them jumped at it. Her business was born and has continued to grow.

That was 15 years ago. Karen was recently named one of the top 10 business women in North Carolina and has even appeared on Oprah's talk show. Karen was patient and kept searching for what she wanted, so when that little spark of inspiration happened, she was ready. She is passionate about her work and that enables her great success.

If you ask yourself what you want and don't get an answer, continue asking. Think about the parameters you want, just like Karen did. And before you know it, that spark of inspiration will appear in your life. Don't forget to act when the inspiration comes. It may be when you least expect it.

Also, keep in mind that you can turn any complaint into a want. In other words, if you are saying, "I don't want to be broke," then the opposite of that complaint is your want, "I want to have money." You can work through this process with any complaint you have. As

Step 5: Nevillize Your Goals

I described in my book, *The Attractor Factor*, your complaints are the springboard to creating your intentions.

Another lesson we can learn from Howard Schultz is to dream big. He once said, "I'd encourage everyone to dream big, lay your foundations well, absorb information like a sponge, and not be afraid to defy conventional wisdom. Just because it hasn't been done before doesn't mean you shouldn't try it."

VISION MAPPING

I encourage everyone to have a Vision Map. This is a tool that helps you constantly keep your vision in front of you. You may have a bulletin board, a notebook, or one of the new vision board software programs that you can download on the Internet. Whatever method you use, they all have the same function. Your Vision Map will have your goals in writing – but that's not enough. You must have a visual tool as well. For example, if you're planning to build your dream home, you should cut out pictures of homes you want and put those on your Vision Map. Then display it in a prominent location, where you can see it every day.

This may feel a little weird at first but it accomplishes several real points. The most important of these is to help you Nevillize what you want. If you are forced to find a picture of what you want, it makes you be very specific and it also allows your mind to easily grasp and imagine the reality of it. It's not just a blurry, half-formed idea, it's a concrete full color rendition of how your life will be.

When you picture your financial success, don't just include photos of piles of money. Insert pictures of how your life will be. Will you drive a Mercedes and live in a three-story house? Put those pictures in. Where will you vacation? Europe? Japan? Australia? Add those as well.

Now here is where your limiting beliefs may start shouting again. You may say, "I'm not talented enough to succeed at that level." But you are. In fact you can increase your talent just as easily as you attract money into your life.

I recently read Daniel Coyle's excellent book *The Talent Code*. The premise of the book is to explain anomalies that produce massive amounts of talent. He notes that there are certain places that have a specific mix of training, motivation, and coaching that produce exceptionally talented people. This finding means that talent isn't necessarily something we're born with. It's something we can create!

The ideas in this book inspired me tremendously and also helped explain some strange events in my own life.

For example, back in 1969 I failed high school geometry. I couldn't tell a parallelogram from an isosceles triangle. I had to retake the course the following year, but this time I got an "A." How did I go from an "F" to an "A?" The answer was that I had a different teacher who intuitively knew the best way to help me learn. This teacher, Mr. Ron Posey, had me follow a strict process. He was extremely specific, all the way down to using a particular notebook, putting protectors around the three holes in the pages, handwriting meticulously, and much more. It drove some students nuts, but it helped me get straight A's. According to Coyle, that second instructor was a brilliant coach intuitively using *The Talent Code's* secrets.

Back in 1972, when I learned how to fly a single-engine plane, I went through a 10-week course. It was the hardest thing I'd ever done. I either flew a plane everyday or was in ground school studying everyday for five days a week, all day long. I thought the curriculum was intense. It wasn't until I read *The Talent Code* that I realized Kent State University's flight school was teaching me exactly the way I needed to learn – by stretching me beyond what I thought was doable. But how does all of this work to increase talent? What were my geometry teacher and that flight school doing to turn a below average kid into a straight A student and a licensed private pilot?

The Talent Code explains the three things needed to increase talent and go toward greatness. One essential element is the spark of inspiration. Something has to ignite your desire, much like viewing that afternoon talk show about an abused child sparked Karen's inspiration to start a business doing nanny background checks.

This spark of inspiration happened to me in 1970 when I met Rod Serling, creator of the famous sci-fi TV series, *The Twilight Zone*. I had always put authors up on a pedestal, but I realized Serling was human and if he could be a famous writer, then I could too. I put myself through a self-study program that contained over 10,000 hours of writing, reading, writing and even more reading. My writings were rejected for years, and yet I tried again and again (and again and again) to be published. My first book wasn't published until 1984. The spark of inspiration was Rod Serling. This "spark" is what begins a huge, deep transformation. It's the way to start unlocking talent. It's interesting that Malcolm Gladwell's book, *Outliers*, confirms this amount of time as key in becoming successful. There is something

Step 5: Nevillize Your Goals

magical about the 10,000-hour mark that pushes a person from trying to being successful.

The amount of practice is the second key ingredient. You can't expect to jump right into success and be able to handle it. You must practice in order to increase your ability and expand in a knowledgeable, sustainable way. Bill Gates didn't jump right into the chairman's seat at Microsoft. He started in his dorm room. Leading up to that point in time, he had also spent untold hours writing code for his vision of a user-friendly computer operating system. He had no magic abilities whatsoever. He created that talent by spending thousands of hours practicing.

The third ingredient is to have a great coach. In the spring of 2009, I took private tutoring lessons with Berlitz instructors to learn Spanish, for a speaking engagement in Lima, Peru. While I had books, courses, and CDs on how to speak Spanish – there's nothing like having a personal coach there to guide my learning. When I failed geometry the first time, but excelled at it the second time, it was due to a better coach. I learned to pilot a plane in a short amount of time, due to great teachers. These days I have my own "Joe Vitale's Miracles Coaching™ program" for people wanting to improve or breakthrough their own barriers. I know from personal experience that a strong coach is needed for success and accomplishment. In fact, it's a requirement.

The great news is that you can develop any talent you want with a combination of these three elements. So don't allow your old beliefs to stand in your way of dreaming big dreams. Just because you may not have the knowledge and skills right now does not mean that you can't attain them in the future. As the subtitle of *The Talent Code* states, "Greatness isn't born. It's grown." So don't ignore that spark of inspiration or the desire of your heart.

Remember, the fifth step is to Nevillize your goal. Want to be financially free forever? Well, what would that feel like? Imagine you're already there. Soak up the good feelings. That's the fifth step and a proven way to program your mind to attract money now.

But we have another two steps to go...

STEP 5: NEVILLIZE YOUR GOALS
TRUTHS & TAKE-AWAYS

- The process of 'Nevillizing' your goal is the fifth step to attracting money.

- When it comes to achieving your goals, you will have greater success if you make the emotional connections in your mind, where you can feel, hear and experience what it will be like to actually have what you're striving for.

- It's your responsibility to act when a source of money is attracted to you.

- Once you understand how powerful Nevillizing is, you'll naturally begin to expand it into every area of your life.

- If you ask yourself what you want and don't get an answer, continue asking.

- Turn your complaints into wants.

- You can't expect to jump right into success and be able to handle it. You must practice in order to increase your ability, and to expand in a knowledgeable and sustainable way.

Step 5: Nevillize Your Goals

ACTION STEPS

- Pick a money goal that excites you and write it down.
- Imagine what it will feel like to have that goal accomplished right now.
- Write a script of your life after that goal has been achieved.

{STEP 6}
THINK LIKE AN ENTREPRENEUR

The best way to attract money is to think like an entrepreneur.
— JOE VITALE

THE REASON YOU WANT to have money is that you want freedom. Freedom to go anywhere, do anything, live as you please and enjoy your life to the fullest. Money gives us the means to make this happen. By far the fastest way to accelerate your income is by becoming an entrepreneur. This doesn't mean just owning a business. The mistake many people make when they own their own business is that they move from working for someone else to working for the business. They don't gain any freedom at all and are tied to the business, as if they were working for a major corporation. They haven't altered their ideas to those of a true entrepreneur.

Entrepreneurs are not interested in having a business to create a job for themselves. They're interested in creating value in as many areas as possible. This means that you will attract revenue in many ways. Some people refer to this as multiple sources of income. The beauty is that once you set it up, it doesn't require much direct involvement on your part to keep bringing in revenue. Books are a good example of this. If you write a book, it sells for years, giving you an ongoing stream of income.

These types of opportunities pop up all the time and if you adopt an entrepreneurial mindset that allows you to see them, and commit to act on them, you may be shocked at what appears. One of my favorite stories is how Fit-a-Rita came about. Fit-a-Rita is a sugar-free, all natural margarita mix that I created. I don't know anything about creating a margarita mix. I do not have a background in food service or any clue how to bring this type of product to market. So how is it that I created a margarita mix?

Step 6: Think Like an Entrepreneur

Several years ago I was competing in a bodybuilding contest and was on a diet where the only beverage I drank was water and I closely watched what I ate. So one night I went out with several other people and they all had mixed drinks while I sipped my ice water. Back then I watched a show on CNBC called *The Big Idea* hosted by Donny Deutsch. He always said that your success is right where your problem is, right where you complain about something. So when you are about to complain about a service, product or need for something, that's when you are telling yourself that there is an opportunity to earn money by fulfilling that need.

So here I am sitting at this dinner wanting a margarita badly! I felt deprived and it just wasn't right! So I said, "Somebody needs to make a healthy bodybuilder's drink, a bodybuilder's margarita mix."

Of course most everyone laughed, but some thought it was a good idea. It was then that the little twinge of inspiration hit and the light bulb went off in my head and I thought, "This *is* a good idea." I had no clue how to start making this a reality, but I had learned to ask. I asked for help. First I talked with a medical doctor and then a nutritionist. We all got together and formed a company – Frontier Nutritional Research. These two professionals helped me compile an ingredient list that was low calorie and healthy for bodybuilders (and anyone else). My contribution during this phase was to be the original taste tester! Not exactly a tough job but I wanted it to taste great. We went through numerous versions until we got one that tasted great and was healthy.

All of this stemmed from one dinner where I wanted a healthy margarita. That problem led me to come up with a solution. You never know where these ideas will lead. If you solve problems you encounter daily, then by default, you'll discover a need that you can profit from.

When you start to think like an entrepreneur you see opportunities everywhere. And you start to create them. This is the sixth step in attracting money into your life. These ideas can be Internet-based, intellectual property (like a book), food products or services. There are all sorts of paths you can follow.

Anyone can learn to think like an entreprenur. As you know, I was once homeless and in poverty, so obviously I had to learn how to think differently. Now I teach others to expand their thinking and look for opportunities. For example, here's a testimonial from someone who just began my Miracles Coaching™ program taught by Prosper Learning (used with permission):

> *It is hard to put into words all the incredible changes Prosper Learning and the Miracles Coaching™ program have helped me achieve.*
>
> *I'd started my journey towards awakening over a year before but subconscious limiting beliefs were holding me back. Joining Prosper is one of the best decisions I've ever made. Working with Janeen Detrick, my personal Prosper coach has allowed me to break through those old beliefs and replace them with new ones. I now know I'm going to be wildly successful. I'm thrilled and perfectly comfortable with that but, here's the best part, I'm already seeing results. I've chosen to start an online business helping clients promote their websites. Before I'd put up my own website, ordered business cards, done any promotion whatsoever or even picked a name for my business, my first client approached me completely out of the blue, hired me on the spot for three months at $500 per month and the following six months at $1500 per month. I'm now officially an entrepreneur and the possibilities are endless!*
>
> *To say it has truly been an amazing experience and an incredibly wise investment would be a huge understatement. Janeen and Prosper have helped me open up the door to the riches of the universe and for that I will be eternally grateful.*
>
> — Adrian McCluskey, British Columbia Canada

THE MILLIONAIRE NEXT DOOR

The vast majority of self-made millionaires weren't born into money. In fact they came from modest backgrounds. What made them millionaires is this entrepreneurial mindset and a very strong drive to succeed.

So here are some questions for you – "How badly do you want to succeed? How strong is that drive to attain the life you say you want?" It can be yours, but you must take the necessary steps for it to happen. Mindset is what separates the financially empowered from those in bondage to their jobs, bills and old expectations. It also separates the modestly successful from the tremendously successful. It could be your neighbor, your friend or even a family member that chooses to understand and use these concepts to change their lives.

Step 6: Think Like an Entrepreneur

In order for you to be a millionaire, you must think constantly about multiple streams of income. I know a pair of fellow writers who make money from books and articles, but also have rental property. They are also investing in a chain of franchise restaurants in Thailand and a cherry orchard in Australia. These two ladies have also partnered with a radio host to produce a group of financial radio shows across Canada and own a percentage of the business generated by an international speaker and lecturer. I asked them how these widely-varied streams of income came about and here is how they described it:

> Well it's interesting to look back on it now, as we never could have guessed we'd be here just three years ago. We're writers and that is really our skill set, so early on we did a few deals with people we thought had great promise to trade our skills for something they needed. There was a radio host who wanted to write a book so we did that for him as well as his second book and agreed to own a percentage of his business in lieu of payment. Now he's hit it big with this new radio show and so have we, as we now are part of the production team. Another person we did a similar agreement with, was a man who was trying to get on the national speaking circuit. We helped with his book and in return, a percentage of his speaking fees come to us.
>
> When we started doing better and had some cash, we wanted to look at ideas that would bring us income and also help others. Anyone can park their money in the stock market but we wanted to do something different and help other entrepreneurs. We heard about a chef who was starting a franchise of little restaurants in Thailand and we thought it was a great idea because it gave the local people an opportunity to work toward owning their own restaurant after the tsunami devastated the area. The cherry orchard came about from an Australian Realtor that we helped with a book. She told us that some of the farmers near her parent's house were reclaiming old vineyards to produce cherries which are in short supply in the southern hemisphere during their summer. We just liked the idea and provided some financing and we continue to look for ideas that help us diversify and keep attracting money.

There are a couple of interesting points about this story that I want to talk about. First, they were looking for opportunities even before they had cash flowing in. They were willing to trade skills they had for future streams of income. This can be beneficial for everyone involved. Relationships created this way are often much more profitable in the long run than they would be if there was just an exchange of cash for service. So don't think you have to have cold hard cash to get started. Be creative and see what happens.

The other item I want to point out is how well diversified these two are. They live in Texas, yet their money comes from the United States, Canada, Thailand and Australia. Don't be afraid to do business around the world. To say you only want to stay within the United States limits your opportunities. It is much like saying, "Yes, I want to attract money but I'll only accept cash." Don't limit yourself. These ladies just followed the leads provided as they came along and it's turned out well for them. Besides they can hop over to Australia to check on the investments and deduct the trip! What a deal!

LET'S TALK MONEY

The whole idea of creating multiple streams of income will have a big impact on your finances. But they don't all have to be big. You may start a stream of income that produces an extra $100 or $200 each month. Is that worth doing? Yes. Not only will you continue to grow this income, but you will add other streams as well. It's not about making a big score every time, but more about diversifying your flow of money so that no matter the economy, or anything that happens in one sector, you'll still have a great income.

Once the money starts flowing, it's easy to forget what a big difference it makes in your life. Let's start with $500. If you earn an additional $500 per month what does that mean? That's an extra $6000 per year that can pay down your debt, provide you a great vacation or go into an investment or enhance a retirement fund. Now that may not sound like a lot, but let's assume that you keep that income stream for five years. Now that's $30,000 – that's a serious chunk of change. One of the mistakes people make is evaluating a stream of income based on a monthly or yearly amount, rather than factoring in the full ongoing amount.

I can't tell you the number of times I've heard really smart people say that owning a rental property isn't worth making a few hundred

Step 6: Think Like an Entrepreneur

per month. Yet that property will be around for years consistently producing income, as well as gaining in value over time. Real estate and many other long-standing solid streams of income are often discounted by those who listen to every piece of bad news on television. They focus on the hassle of getting it going and the risk involved, not the value of the revenue stream.

But I'll be honest with you: I don't care about or even like rental property. Maybe you don't either – but some people do and do very well at it. Keep in mind that you can choose what you are involved in, but you don't have to try something just because someone else is doing it.

How about intellectual property? A book for example.

I've also talked to well-known people who discount the idea of doing a book. They just don't think it's really worth it as you generally don't make much for your first effort. However, if you keep going as I have, the stream of revenue from over 30 books is substantial, and it just keeps flowing without my active intervention.

When you're evaluating a potential source of income, it's important to keep a few things in mind. First, it should be flexible when you're starting out. You may have to work around your full-time job. Flexibility gives you the opportunity to attract money without being tied down to a set schedule or numbers of hours every week.

I also like opportunities that can grow over time. While it's great to get $500 each month, it would be even better if you had the possibility to grow that amount and eventually generate $1,000 or $1,500 per month. Another thing you want to keep in mind is that you want the income to continue. Is it sustainable? You don't want to necessarily put in the time to get the income started if it's only going to last a few months or only a year. This is especially true if that same amount of time and effort could potentially produce the same income stream that continues for years. Eventually, you also want that income stream to function without you having to manage it every day.

It's vital that you do what you love. This is why I suggest you look at your hobbies as potential ways to produce income. You enjoy these already or they wouldn't be your hobbies. One of the worst things you can do is get into a business that you don't like just to make money. Your emotions will inhibit your ability to attract money because you don't really like the business in the first place. After a while it will feel like a weight around your neck and you'll dread it. This is not a formula for success. Go with what you love and the money will follow.

While you can pony up the big bucks for a number of business opportunities, why do that if you don't have to? I like ideas that cost little or no money to start. This means that if you're willing to work hard, you will make a profit from the very first dollar and you won't have to carry any debt or worry about making payments. The idea is to achieve freedom and that's more difficult to do if you saddle yourself with additional responsibilities and debts.

I know a lady named Janet who was laid off from her executive assistant position a couple of years ago. There were few opportunities and she was tired of commuting from her suburban home in Florida to downtown Miami to work. She took stock of her skill set and found it extensive. She read an article on the Internet about virtual assistants who work part time for several executives and communicate by phone and email. Janet now works from home and has two other assistants working for her who also work from home. She makes more money than she ever did being physically in the office and gets much more work done without the commute and distraction of co-workers who used to walk into her office just to chat. Janet is a good example of someone who basically loved her job, but it just wasn't working well for her. Now she can use those same skills and still provide a valuable service to her clients.

I see numerous people who think they have to look at something totally different than their current job to attract money but it's just not true. I know a man named Jerry who loved his job at the hospital in Taos, New Mexico. Because he'd struggled with post traumatic stress in the past and had gone through training to counsel others, he soon became a post traumatic stress consultant to the hospital staff members. He quickly realized the need for knowledgeable people to help medical human resource departments deal with this issue. Jerry has retired from his normal floor duties and now gives seminars all across the state to medical organizations and conferences on how to cope with post traumatic stress on the job. He also is working on an informational seminar. It will be available online soon for other hospital administrators. They will then be able to learn what they should do when faced with individuals suffering from post traumatic stress.

Both of these examples meet most of the requirements for great sources of income. And they keep producing, capitalizing on the Internet.

Step 6: Think Like an Entrepreneur

THE INTERNET IS YOUR FRIEND

Many people know me from my appearance as the star of the movie, *The Secret*, but few really know that I started my career as an Internet marketer. Back in 1995 I wrote one of the few Internet marketing books that existed. In fact I wrote several books on general marketing as well. So believe me I know the power of the Internet. I also know that it can give you enough business to change your life.

The Internet is really unique because it's used by almost every person living in developed countries around the world. It's easy to access, costs little, and can put you in touch with customers all over the world. It gives you the opportunity to start small and then grow your business. You can have a business in conjunction with your day job while building your income. Doing business online also gives you the option of spending more time with your children and family. For this reason alone, many people with small children choose to pursue this avenue.

The ability to do keyword searches on Google can also give you valuable information on what people are really interested in. This is more difficult if you're starting another type of business. But online information for Internet businesses is readily available. The range and type of opportunity on the Internet is vast, allowing you to match your passion and what you enjoy doing with what is available. Many of these opportunities are non-traditional. I know a stay-at-home mom who loves to play poker. She plays online and now has a very successful poker blog. She contributes online poker articles to one of the major poker Internet sites and gets numerous paid trips to Las Vegas to cover high-level poker events. Now this is a soccer mom from Dallas who has no interest in moving her children to Las Vegas or living a gambling lifestyle, but she can still make money off her world-class skill right from home. None of the opportunities she enjoys were an option as recent as 10 years ago. New and different options are surfacing everyday. You can take advantage of them, as long as you're open to the possibilities.

Most people have at least one or two things in their lives that they're deeply passionate about. Perhaps it's cooking or pets. Maybe it is gardening or writing. If you have a true passion for something, it's well worth your time to try to investigate the online opportunities and see if you can turn that passion and talent into some additional income – or perhaps a new career.

You've heard me mention my blog several times. Blogs are free and if you develop a following, advertisers will want to pay you to place their ads on your website. This is probably the number one way that bloggers make money on the Internet. Now blogging takes discipline as well as the ability to communicate. So if these are qualities you possess, then it might suit you. Once you start looking you can find blogs on any subject and you can write one on anything. I encourage you to write about something interesting that helps people. These attract the most readers. You may help people grow home gardens, fix up their home, eliminate their debt and become financially secure, or whatever else fits your passion. Just be sure you can post at least a couple of times every week or even every day.

Another area that has really taken off on the Internet is virtual learning. This doesn't necessarily mean formal education. People take online classes to learn everything from English to novel writing. All you need is to be passionate and knowledgeable and you can turn that into an online course. I invented the e-class way back in the late 1990s. Lessons and lectures can be sent each week to students who may return their homework via email. Many people who used to teach classes in a seminar or classroom setting have moved to the Internet as it offers low overhead and you can maintain larger numbers of students from all over the world. There aren't any geographical limitations. Tutoring can also be lucrative in the online realm and many schoolteachers use this avenue to enhance their teaching income during the school year and then add income during the summer.

Since the introduction of YouTube, online videos have exploded. Now many businesses and even authors are using videos to sell their product. If you have the skills to create and edit these types of videos, there are numerous opportunities online. I know of a young couple (he was a television news producer and she was a school teacher), and when their daughter was born, they decided that it would be more practical for him to quit his job and stay home to produce sales and training videos for businesses. Now he earns more than he did working 70 hours per week at the television station and he gets to enjoy seeing their daughter grow.

Even teenagers these days have significant video production skills. So don't think that age is a limitation. This holds true for any online business. Your customers have no clue if you're 19 or even 85, so there aren't any preconceived notions. You are treated as a professional as long as you act like one. So use that to your advantage.

Step 6: Think Like an Entrepreneur

One area that almost needs its own category is eBay. Thousands of people use online auctions to generate additional income. You can sell items lying around your house or you may purchase items in bulk and auction them off. You can even have one of their online storefronts that generate orders. These are extremely simple to set up and maintain. There is a lady named Maureen who got into this line of business. She was trying to sell off items from her aunt's estate. It went so well, she now advertises in her local newspaper to buy whole estates and then sell the items online.

There's really no excuse for not investigating the various possibilities you have to earn additional income from the Internet. While it's not the only way, it is certainly one of the easiest and most inexpensive ways to get one of your streams of income. This will allow you to start attracting money immediately.

Remember, the sixth step to attract money now is to think like an entrepreneur. Anyone can learn to do this. When I was starting out as a writer, I didn't have a clue how to think like that. I was also broke. As I learned to see and act on opportunities everywhere, my happiness and income grew by leaps and bounds.

We have one more step for attracting money now. If you're ready, just turn the page.

STEP 6: THINK LIKE AN ENTREPRENEUR
TRUTHS & TAKE-AWAYS

- The sixth step to attracting money is to think like an entrepreneur.

- In order for you to be a millionaire, you must set up multiple streams of income.

- Choose opportunities that will grow over time.

- It's vital that you do what you love. Look at your hobbies as potential ways to produce income.

- Most people have one or two things that they're deeply passionate about – turn these into your first opportunities.

- There's no excuse for not investigating the various possibilities for additional income that you can attract through the Internet.

- Anyone can learn to think and act like an entrepreneur.

Step 6: Think Like an Entrepreneur

ACTION STEPS

- Write down 10 things you love to do.
- Consider which one you could turn into a product or service.
- Write down ways you could sell your product or service online.
- Take action today to make it happen.

{STEP 7}
HELP YOUR COMMUNITY AND YOUR WORLD

I resolved to stop accumulating and begin the infinitely more serious and difficult task of wise distribution.
— ANDREW CARNEGIE

IF THERE IS ONE CONCEPT that I must get across to you it is that we are not alone. I don't mean that little green men will land in your backyard, but that we as humans are connected to one another – and what we do, think and feel affects others. **The seventh and final step to attracting money is caring for your community and the world as a whole.**

I recently saw a show on the History Channel that taught the history of the prison system. In the late 1800s several large prisons were built in the United States. The idea behind these prisons wasn't reform; it was punishment. The prisoners were kept in absolute solitude for years on end. This drove legions of prisoners insane and lead to solitary confinement being regarded as the highest level of punishment.

Humans are social creatures and we can't exist without contact with others. We are formed of the same substance and we connect with one another constantly. This affords us special opportunities. As we learn and experience personal growth and success, we can't help having an impact on everyone around us. As one person is raised up, it naturally lifts those around them, while providing inspiration and hope.

When you view everyone as interconnected, you'll realize that as you attract more money into your life, you have the opportunity to effect change in others. This is the seventh and final step to attracting money – caring for your community and the world. This works hand-in-hand with giving – but it's not just about money. It's about sharing your time, knowledge and the lessons you've learned. Your success is a

Step 7: Help Your Community and Your World

great catalyst for doing good in the world. I'm constantly looking for ways to give back, as well as connect with others in meaningful ways.

Due to the time I spent homeless, I find homelessness a crisis that's very close to my heart. I know it can happen to anyone because I experienced it firsthand. I wanted to do something to help. I didn't want to simply offer food or clothing. There are many charities that already meet those needs. What I wanted to do was something that could help people rescue themselves financially by teaching them the techniques and skills to be financially successful. It's called Operation YES. YES stands for Your Economic Salvation and is a project that I'm working on with several partners. Our mission is to end homelessness and stop foreclosures.

The spark for Operation YES arrived like every other inspiration I've had. Here's the story. I heard about the economic stimulus package that was offered several years ago. The government decided to give out checks for $300 or $600 to everyone. I heard this and thought, "That's a nice thought but it's not going to make a real difference." I figured that most people would buy clothes, pay a bill or even pay down some debt. But it wasn't going to change their lives or help them become financially sound. As I was sitting there, I thought, "You know, someone should do something that really makes a difference." And that's when it hit me like a bolt of lightning. Why not me? I'm someone. I know enough about how hard it is to start your life over from nothing. Why couldn't I do something? So I did.

I figured that if I can teach people to raise their self-esteem, then they'd have a real chance to improve their life. Self-esteem is important when you're on the bottom rung of life. You feel like a failure. You feel like the lowest most insignificant person alive. But you're not! It's just your perception and mindset of the moment. Those who are both broke and homeless suffer from a double whammy. Operation YES teaches people how to rebuild their self-esteem, so they have hope, can feel worthwhile and that they can accomplish positive things.

Once the homeless have recovered their self-esteem, I teach them about the Law of Attraction and how they can attract anything they want, including money and opportunities. Operation YES shows people that this basic rule of psychology can change their lives permanently and they won't have to worry about ending up on the streets again. I tell them that what they focus on will increase or expand. This means if they focus on being homeless and broke, they will get more of that in their lives. Unfortunately most people who live on the street only focus on survival.

In order to see the opportunity to improve their lives, they must think differently while focusing on a new and better life. They must use the Law of Attraction and see their end result, not the reality of the moment. They have to stop and think about what they want. This seems obvious to you and me, but how often do average people with the house, dog, two cars and three kids stop to think about their lives? We are creatures of habit with comfort zones. And we stay in them, even if our comfort zones produce negative results. It can happen to anyone.

The third level of Operation YES is to teach the homeless entrepreneurial skills, much like the ones I've described in this book. They can work for anyone from a bank president to a homeless person. I'm living proof that these skills work. The ones who really understand these principles, know they can generate income from pursuing things they love rather than trying to eke out a living flipping burgers or bagging groceries for someone else. They can create their own lives, their own incomes, and never be dependent on anyone else ever again.

I choose to help the planet by helping those in severe need. You may choose a very different avenue but it's important that you participate in your community and your world because whatever you send out will come back to you. Emotions of goodwill and love for people you don't know, will create tremendous flow of those same emotions back to you. It's an awe-inspiring thing to see.

When you start to think bigger than yourself and what you want, you release the limitations from your life that were blocking more money from coming your way. You may be wondering why this has any effect on money. Money is only one resource, as is love, caring and abundance. It is our own human beliefs that separate the ideas of human kindness and charity from money. Some think that money and pure altruism cannot exist together. Not only do they exist together – they're intertwined. The resource of money is not separate.

If you don't care about the people around you or treat them as if they don't matter, you'll stop the flow of possibilities. This includes your financial prosperity. Creating a vehicle for good that you feel passionate about is the final step toward true prosperity.

Step 7: Help Your Community and Your World

YOU CONTROL THE UNIVERSE

I enjoyed a moderate amount of success before I completely understood these principles. In fact, what really started my journey of intense personal growth, and what motivates me to continue, is my intrigue with how some people overcome negative and hopeless situations to succeed and others don't. I've come all the way from the streets to a really nice life, yet I couldn't really verbalize or explain how it happened. This concerned me. I was afraid if I didn't know what caused my success, I might lose it.

Of course I now know that the reason I succeeded without really understanding the power of the Law of Attraction was that I figured it out intuitively and used it unconsciously. I was determined to try anything, and through trial and error, some things worked, so I continued to do them. It wasn't until later I understood about asking, or giving or any of the concepts that are an integral part of true and lasting success.

I realized that when I focused on what I really want, I would attract it. When I was stressed and worried about my situation, things got worse. I'm not a fan of pain and suffering, so I went with what worked. It wasn't until later that I realized the awesome power our minds possess. It's a little scary that I just wielded that power willy-nilly at one time. Now I'm aware and it's this awareness that allows a higher form of knowledge to flow through me, allowing me to accomplish things that I never could've on my own.

If we believe something to exist, so it is. Now those words really underscore the power you have within you. You shape the world you live in and have the power to reshape it. Yet so many people waste this power on habitual thoughts and old beliefs that originated with others. Changing your thoughts alone will not produce your desired results. You must also take inspired action. The awareness that you are connected to a tremendous source of power will guide your actions. There is a great exercise that really illustrates the power of your mind and how a new mindset can be the catalyst for tremendous change.

Imagine that you're in a dark room where every comfort has been provided to you. The room is completely dark preventing you from reaching out for those things you desire. You were told that the room has lights, so you instinctively grope along the wall, where you're accustomed to finding a switch.

For many hours you pass your hands up and down the walls as far as you can reach until your arms ache. About the time you're ready to give up the search, you keep going, determined to locate the switch. You're determined to enjoy the good things awaiting you, so you sustain your search, knowing that you'll ultimately find a way to turn on the light.

After more searching, you pause to rest. You wonder where that switch could possibly be. "It must be here, and I will find it," you say to yourself, and again you pass your hands over the walls, although you feel certain that you've already gone over every inch of wall within your reach. This time your thoughts and movements are not quite so tense, although equally determined. As your hands move slowly up and down, your mind sparks the idea that the switch might not be on the wall at all. You pause for a moment. Next, you think that the switch might be on the floor. But reason steps in and argues, "Impossible. Who ever heard of a light switch being placed on the floor!"

"But," the suggestion persists, "why not try? You've gone over everywhere you thought it would be. What the heck, try the floor."

Then you reach out across the floor with your foot hoping to find something feeling like a light switch. Instantly your toes brush against an unfamiliar object. You put your hand on what seems to be a push button, but no light appears. Nevertheless, you now feel quite *sure* that you've located the switch.

Pause, and ask yourself, "How does this thing work? It won't push and it won't pull." Back comes the answer within yourself, like a spoken word. "Sideways." You move it sideways, and the room is flooded with light. Your joy at finding a responsive intelligence within yourself cannot be expressed in words. It is a rapture of the heart that many others have felt at various times.

This story is a mirror of how holding onto the correct mindset helps you meet your goals. At first you reach out for what you know, and the answer is not there. It's at that point you begin to search and open yourself to other ideas. Even when you encounter obstacles and become frustrated, you still search for answers. The answer comes to you from what seems like thin air, but it's the universal intelligence helping you reach your goals and giving you the answers. This is because you stayed focused on your goal.

Now imagine yourself in the same room under the same conditions. After several attempts at feeling around in the dark, you feel tired, more or less discouraged, and you reason with yourself, "Oh, what is the use? There *may* be a light switch in this room, and

Step 7: Help Your Community and Your World

the room *may* contain everything I require and again it *may* not." But something indefinable within yourself convinces you that not only is the light there, but so are the things you enjoy and desire. You say, "Well, if everything I enjoy is here, what a pity that I *cannot* find the switch! I wonder why the light was not already turned on for me."

This is a typical reaction for many people. They say, "It's not my fault, it's the crazy mixed-up world we live in! It's my family, my boss, the President and I can't help it." They blame everyone and everything when they have the ability to overcome the issue – but refuse to understand that they already possess that power.

Once you recognize that there's a universal intelligence that can and will respond, you also understand your own responsibility to act on it. Just like being in the dark room, you had to act in order to find the answer. Even when you didn't have a clue why things weren't working or what might work. You must keep trying and wait for the spark of intuitive intelligence to appear.

PERSISTENCE OF WILL

You must never quit. I encounter people everyday who seem to have QUIT tattooed on their foreheads. It's as if they have made up their minds way in advance that they will give a new idea X amount of effort and that's it. They may decide that rather than 100% effort they will give 95%, but usually it's more like 30% or 40%. They don't really want to commit, so when they fail, they have a ready-made excuse. They can distance themselves from becoming emotionally attached to the outcome.

We all have our low points or our own personal 'crises of faith.' Persistence is the ability to maintain your action and outlook regardless of your feelings. You press on even when you feel like quitting. When you work toward any big goal, it's normal for your motivation to ebb and flow like waves hitting the beach.

Sometimes you'll feel motivated; sometimes you won't. But it's your action that will produce results. Persistence allows you to keep taking inspired action, even when you don't feel motivated. Then you still produce results. Over time, persistence will enhance your motivation, as the quest becomes almost like a puzzle you must solve. It's just like trying to find the light switch. The persistence to keep looking and thinking of other possibilities will motivate you far beyond your limits. If you keep taking inspired action, you'll eventually get results. These results will continue to motivate you. For example, you may become much more excited about attracting money when you go to your mailbox and find a check you didn't expect.

Persistence doesn't mean you blindly stumble forward no matter what. You must be willing to step back and evaluate your progress and stay on the path toward your goals. Persistence means you keep searching for answers and plugging away consistently at your dreams. Persistence is not stubbornness and this can be a difficult lesson to learn. Many people were raised to believe that once you set a goal you should stick with it and go down with the ship if necessary. This is why people stay in jobs they hate, live for years in a location they don't care for and spend their time with people they don't like. They are living in guilt – not persistence.

As you grow, your dreams and desires will change. They will grow and morph into something way beyond what you can imagine. When I was studying at Kent State to become a journalist, I never imagined that several decades later I'd be speaking to more than 17,000 people in Lima, Peru or scale the heights of Machu Picchu – but I did.

Speaking of Peru, I spoke there because of two young entrepreneurs named Raul and Hugo. These men live in a third-world country, yet they dream BIG. They wanted me to speak to their country. At first their goal was to have me speak to 35,000 people and meet the President of Peru. Sometimes, things change as you make progress to your dreams. Instead of speaking to 35,000 people, I spoke to 17,000. Instead of meeting the President of Peru, I met with television reporters that promoted me to the entire country. Raul and Hugo kept their vision while they took inspired action and adapted the event as new information became available. Meeting them was a thrill. And speaking to the crowd they gathered was one of the highlights of my life. I expect even bigger things to come.

My dreams have grown and changed and so will yours. You can't guarantee that the goals you set today will still be the ones you want to achieve a year from now. In order to make room for new goals, we have to delete or finish old ones. Sometimes you'll get a spark that's so compelling and inspiring, that there's no way to go back and finish your old one. They may have to be abandoned half-finished. I've always found it uncomfortable to do this, but I know it's necessary to follow that intuitive spark. Let go of the idea that you must complete everything you start because sometimes what you learn partway through that one idea, leads to an even better one. Follow the lead of intuition and it will show you how to discern the true path.

Step 7: Help Your Community and Your World

Mark was a closet writer when I met him. He worked in a local accounting firm and had dreams of publishing a book to help college kids learn basic financial principles. He worked on it on and off for years and everyone in his life knew he'd been working on this book forever and doubted that it would ever be finished. Finally a college administrator walked into his office. After talking a bit, the conversation turned to how much of a need there is to teach young people how to handle money. Mark told the administrator that he was working on a book about it. The administrator asked if he'd be interested in teaming up and co-authoring the book.

Mark had a decision to make. Did he set aside his dream, or did he seize this opportunity? After some thinking about it, Mark decided that taking the co-authoring opportunity was the right decision. The book was published a year later and met with success due to the backing of Mark's coauthor and the university he worked for. Mark was soon out lecturing and teaching his passion to young people, an opportunity that might have languished and disappeared if he hadn't been willing to alter his dream.

These days I set very big goals. I want to receive all there is out there. Does this mean that I set out on a path only to hop on another one when an opportunity presents itself? Yes! I have lots of different ideas and opportunities that come my way. In the early years I had a hard time deciding which ones I was supposed to take. I'd get these 'gut' feelings like most people do, then I would try and "logic" my way through it. Needless to say I spent a lot of time on things that were a waste of time. I learned the hard way.

These days I've learned to trust my intuition. Sometimes it's an emotional connection to the idea or maybe just a feeling about a person's potential. I talk to other personal development leaders everyday. There are a few that I will work with someday. I just know it intuitively. Over time you'll also develop this ability to know which opportunities to choose and which to turn down.

INSPIRE OTHERS

I read about inspiring people all the time. I like being inspired and I want to be an inspiration to others. This is one of the leading ways to help improve the lives of people you don't know. We all have people who inspire us. But how do you inspire others? I think the first way is to be a good role model. People will watch what you do more than listen to what you say you're going to do. So in order to inspire people, you must do what you say you're going to do. It's sad but sometimes true that the more successful you become, the more people will come out of nowhere to tear you down. You can't be distracted by this noise. As long as you hold true to your principles, you will prove them wrong every time. And as you move forward, more supportive people will be attracted to you and your success.

I've heard it said (heck I've even said it!) that people don't care what you know until they know how much you care. You can't swoop in and tell people what they have to do, how to do it, and expect them to listen. You can see this in today's high school classrooms. Kids aren't impressed by credentials or awards. They want to know if you care about them. Until you show that you care, they won't listen to a word you say. Adults are the same way. Take the time to make a personal connection with people before you offer any advice. Ask questions and take a genuine interest.

Everyone goes through tough times. You've probably seen people that refuse to acknowledge that they've ever had a bad day. Don't be one of them. Encourage those who need a kind word, no matter how difficult their situation may be. Don't be afraid to share your tough memories and experiences. Those who are struggling often feel alone. They feel like nobody else has ever had it so bad. Let them know they aren't alone.

Writers often talk about 'filling the well.' This is a reference to the fact that you can't be inspiring to others unless you get inspired yourself. I read many inspiring stories, blogs and watch inspiring programs and films to get and stay inspired. Look for people, ideas, environments and knowledge that you find inspiring and motivating.

It's very important for you to become a great communicator, so you can get your message across to others. Listen to how you speak, as well as analyze the things you say to people. I've invested plenty of time and money to improve my communication skills.

Always increase your knowledge. Nobody knows everything about anything. Learning and growing is an important part of becoming the type of person you want to evolve into. Learning from others is key, so listen to audio seminars or attend live events. Get books and read them. Don't just stick them in the 'to be read' pile (I know that trick!). Actually read, understand and act on them.

I like to challenge people. It's an obligation I take very seriously. This doesn't mean I'm confrontational. I simply challenge people to get to the next level. This is where I got the nickname "Mr. Fire!" A

Step 7: Help Your Community and Your World

friend said I was always setting "a fire" under people to get them to follow their dreams. Well, I'm here to fire *you* up now.

I like to ask people hard questions regarding what they're doing to make their dreams come true. I also want to know why they're doing it. I do this in every book or program that I produce. On occasion, when I'm tired or really drained, I may sit next to a person on a plane and never say a word. It will usually cross my mind that I may have been put in that seat because the person next to me needed me to ask about their life and challenge them to expand their thinking. When that thought occurs, I speak.

Remember, the seventh and final step to attracting money is caring for your community and the world as a whole. I always want to be the person who inspires others, who cares and who makes a difference. You can do the same.

Now let's put all seven steps together so you can begin to attract money now.

STEP 7: HELP YOUR COMMUNITY & YOUR WORLD TRUTHS & TAKE-AWAYS

- The seventh and final step to attracting money is caring for your community and the world as a whole.
- Emotions of goodwill and love for people you don't even know, creates tremendous flow of those same emotions back to you.
- You shape the world you live in and have the power to reshape it.
- In order to get what you want in life, you must resolve to never quit.
- It's not your motivation that will produce results — it's your inspired action.
- As you grow, your dreams and desires will change – don't be afraid to jump on new opportunities that inspire you.
- In order to inspire others, you must allow yourself to be inspired.

Step 7: Help Your Community and Your World

ACTION STEPS

- Write down causes or movements you care about.
- Find a way to help one of those causes or movements.
- Write down a person you know of who needs help.
- Find a way to help that person.

THE FREEDOM TO LIVE!

Focusing your life solely on making a buck shows a certain poverty of ambition. It asks too little of yourself. Because it's only when you hitch your wagon to something larger than yourself, that you realize your true potential.
— **BARACK OBAMA**

IF YOU WON THE LOTTO for, say, $37 million, what would you do?

Yes, you'll buy the fancy car (or two), a big house (or two), and go on a world travel exotic vacation (or two).

But after that – after you've explored the world and bought all the ice cream you could eat – what will you do?

Those who have achieved their goals are free to live a lifestyle that most people don't even know exists. They aren't held by national borders or boundaries and move freely around the globe without the financial limitations and restrictions of others. The ultimate freedom is to never worry about where money is coming from. It just flows to you.

Occasionally we get a glimpse of this type of life when we see jet-setting celebrities. But most of those living a truly free life aren't like the celebrities, instead they are quiet and unassuming. They have achieved everything they ever dreamed of and now spend their time enjoying every aspect of the world we live in and help millions of people around the globe.

The fear and uncertainty that many people feel is not relevant to their income stream. Fortunes were made in every recession ever to hit the United States. As we move more toward an ever-increasing global economy, new and upcoming entrepreneurs have a view toward opportunity – no matter where it comes from. The old days of only being able to attract income in a local area are gone. Now the world awaits us (you and me), as Internet access has connected us, people from all around the world, and opened up infinite creative possibilities.

The principles that I've outlined in *Attract Money Now* will catapult you into this type of life. And it all starts with your thinking. You have to figure out where you are in your thought process right now. What limiting beliefs are standing in your way? Where did they come from and how do they affect you?

When I read a book or listen to an audio recording that really hits home, I take a few minutes to really think about what the author said. Do that now. Are you willing to release the emotions you've attached to money? Are you ready to release what you think it says about you? Let it go right now. Start at the beginning and make a decision to follow every step I've laid out, so you can receive the abundance and financial rewards that await you.

Start with your thinking. Be aware of all the negativity you're immersed in every day. It comes from movies, conversation, newspapers, and negative people. Give yourself a break from this constant stream of depressing news and fill your mind with positive, uplifting concepts. Pay attention to the three thieves and become aware of how these old beliefs rob you of your future.

Everyone thinks they understand money. Few really do. You can step into the flow of wealth and abundance as easily as you can step out of it. This is the difference between a life of wonder, where you attract as much or more money than you need, and a life of struggle and heartache. Always remember that you can choose to step into the flow at any point as long as you want to. There's no magic formula or secret decoder ring. Membership is open to anyone who wants to join!

I remember a friend of mine asking a wealthy person how he felt about taking risks in business. The wealthy man said, "I don't take risks." He went on to explain that he knows money is like a river. He simply goes to the river and fills his bucket. If he happens to spill some water – or lose some money – he just goes back to the river and refills his bucket. Where's the river? It's in his MIND.

Please don't forget to give. Tithe 10% of your income and then take the next step and give beyond what you've ever given before. Open the door wide to start the flow and circulation of money through your life. Don't forget that you'll receive in direct proportion to what you give – so give a lot!

Never deprive yourself of the things you want due to fear or guilt. Buy that new car or fancy lighter if you choose! (Don't go into debt or tap out your credit cards, though.) Life is to be enjoyed at every level, even if you don't have $1 million in the bank. No matter where you are financially, the way you spend your money now will be reflected in what comes to you later. And while you're responsible to dig yourself out of whatever mess you are in, your attitude and how you choose to spend your money will determine what's attracted to you. Choose to spend in those areas that give you pleasure and create positive emotions, while you're getting your finances in order.

Asking for help will jump start your dreams. Don't hesitate to ask for help on your journey. Ask your mentors, as well as those who've achieved what you want to achieve. A mastermind group is a great way to get the support and ideas you need to get your new ideas and ventures off the ground. Everyone wants the honor of being asked to help, so don't hold out and try to do everything yourself. You'll accomplish much more in less time if you accept help from others. Asking the Divine, God or the Universe for help is also a great avenue to increase your financial circulation. It gives you an emotional release and opens your mind to new and different opportunities.

As you define your goals, spend time each day Nevillizing them. Imagine what it will be like when you accomplish each and create an emotional connection. Hold this connection in your mind and feel the emotions. This positive outpouring speeds up the process. The more connected you are to your end result, the more focus, drive and creativity you'll have in completing it. When you have your goals in mind, think like an entrepreneur. See the options all around you to generate or increase the flow of money.

We are social creatures, whom need contact, support and caring from others. As you grow, you'll have the opportunity to uplift everyone around you by sharing your experiences and ideals. Don't overlook this opportunity to help those who need it most. Remember that you were helped too. This will increase your circulation to the highest level, and it will allow you to have a positive impact on the world.

EXIST IN GRATITUDE

Everyday, I take time to say thanks and express my gratitude for the gifts and opportunities I receive. The expression of gratitude is a liberating release of powerful emotion that you send out into the universe. As we've discussed, the stronger the emotion you attach to something, the more likely you'll get an abundance of it in return.

Think and Grow Rich, by Napoleon Hill, *As A Man Thinketh* by James Allen and the *Science of Getting Rich* by Wallace D. Wattles, are brilliant works emphasizing the importance of gratitude. The most successful people constantly express their humble and sincere gratitude.

The value of gratitude does not solely exist for getting more in the future. Without gratitude, you'll inevitably be dissatisfied with things. The moment you permit your mind to become dissatisfied with your current circumstances, you'll lose ground and slide back into your old ways. If you fix your attention on the negative circumstances in your life, that focus will stop the flow of money and other good things that can help you. This can be a vicious cycle. Existing in a mindset filled with gratitude keeps you positive.

Whatever we focus on – we attract. Focus on the positive and be grateful. Bigger and better things will come your way. When you dwell on the negative and inferior or the worst-case scenario, you're sending negativity out and will continually attract negative results. On the other hand, if you focus on the positives in your life and express sincere gratitude, you'll attract better circumstances. This is an unaltered, permanent law of being, that is at work all the time. There's no pause, stop or rewind. You can become aware of the power of gratitude and work with it for your personal benefit. Or you can deny this power and work against it, which will provide negative results.

It's necessary for us to deliberately and intentionally form the habit of being aware of and grateful for every good thing that comes to us. Then we have to continually give thanks. It's reported that Albert Einstein said "thank you" hundreds of times a day to his predecessors and the Universe, recognizing the inspiring and creative thoughts that came to him daily. Einstein understood the power and benefits of being grateful. You can use this power to fill each day with positive emotions.

Express gratitude for everything that has come to you throughout your lifetime. You even need to express gratitude for the hard times, negative events and bad hair days. Why? Because these were lessons (big and small) that you've benefited from.

In addition to being grateful for what you have now, you can also send thanks for things that will happen to you. I call this "Thanking Forward." "Thanking Forward" is being grateful in advance, as if you already have what you want before it shows up. It's a Nevillization of gratitude!

Scientific studies have consistently proven that significant achievements are reached after just 30 days of Nevillizing (or visualizing with feeling the end result) a goal, event or material thing. Stop and think about what you've done over the past 30 days? Did it go by in the wink of an eye? Now, I want you to imagine your goal over the next 30 days and see the difference it'll make in your life.

Express your gratitude in the morning often before you get out of bed, during the day and after you lay down to go to sleep. All of this will shift the energy you're sending out, and even more significantly, the energy you're attracting into your life. It's not a complicated or difficult process, nor should it seem like work. I like to express my gratitude from my hot tub each evening. It doesn't really matter when, where or how you do this – just that you do it.

If you're not used to expressing gratitude, you may need to adjust your schedule and set aside a few minutes throughout the day to do it. You may even need to put a reminder up on the bathroom mirror, kitchen refrigerator or your computer. Shortly after, you'll do this naturally and find yourself consistently sending out positive gratitude thoughts. In turn, you'll receive astounding results from every direction. Do this process intentionally until it becomes habit. You'll be amazed at how quickly people, events and circumstances will be naturally attracted to you, as well as how quickly your financial circumstances change for the better.

Gratitude can transform your mindset from focusing on you to focusing on others. As we previously discussed early on – when you focus on others, you open yourself up to a tremendous amount of circulation. Saying thanks for everyone in your life and the events that have transpired work together to keep you constantly aware that you need others. We're all connected and cherish feeling appreciation.

THE POWER OF NOW

Have you ever noticed that just about every TV infomercial ends with a call to action? They all seem to say, "Don't wait, act now!" This phrase is just as applicable to you. Waiting to take advantage of an opportunity is a way to cheat yourself from attracting additional income. Don't put it off or put this book down and think, "That's a great idea, I'll work on it when I have time." You already have time, but you're filling it with tasks that aren't really a number one priority. There's no better time than the present.

You're 100% responsible for your life and peace of mind. If you don't have peace of mind, you're wallowing in old limiting beliefs that

The Freedom to Live!

are not serving you. You must get your beliefs in order, so that you can attract money into your life.

All the money in the world will not give you peace of mind. So many people, maybe you, live in financial chaos. How many celebrities or wealthy people do you hear about who die sad and alone because they never found peace of mind? No other person can give you peace. Running to teachers and gurus for answers will not give you peace. Moving to a different location will not give you peace. Peace does not come from outside you. It's obtained within you. The answers that you long for, are already part of you. You just need to understand and practice them. Then you will lead the life you've been longing for. Attaining peace is as simple as this: Give peace and you'll receive peace.

By the same token, if you express gratitude daily, you'll receive astounding rewards. The key is that you are thankful and express gratitude every moment of every day. Always turn the other cheek against adversity and misfortune. You must wish success on everyone else and show them love.

Many people take the idea of giving to mean that whatever they send out comes back like a boomerang. While this is true for the most part, it doesn't mean that it will come back from the same source or in a scheduled amount of time. It only states that you will receive equal (usually ten times more) to what you have given. This applies to money, time, gratitude and caring.

How often does a person truly give without the thought of getting something in return? When you give love, you expect love. When you give understanding to someone you expect someone to be understanding of you. When you give a gift you usually expect a gift back. You may even expect that the person you gave the gift to will like or respect you even more. Unfortunately, very few people will just give from the heart.

When some people don't receive what they expected, or more, they have a tendency to feel hurt, hostile and even angry. Some twist things around and will quickly say that the Law of Attraction doesn't work and call it a sham. I feel sorry for these people. The anger and hostility are blocking their ability to attract, so they have no option other than spiraling downward. They will settle for a mediocre life at best.

Sometimes you may feel like you don't have a choice as to how your life will turn out. You do!

One of my favorite scenes comes from the classic movie *The Wizard of Oz*. After the trials and tribulations that Dorothy faced on her journey, she still hasn't found her way home. Glinda, the Good Witch of the North, tells Dorothy that she has always had the power inside her to get home. All she had to do was wish for it and she would return to her loved ones. I've always found this to be very symbolic of the journey many people take when they seek success. They try hard, only to find that it was as simple as a thought. There is an old saying, "To Think Is to Create." This is how you start changing your life. You must be able to imagine it. Then you'll attract the resources for it to come into being.

So begins your journey of ultimate freedom. My friend and business colleague Peter Wink is another great example of this. Peter had been dating many women for years, never finding Ms. Right. Finally fed up one day, he wrote down exactly what he was looking for in a woman. He wrote down exactly how she would look, talk, and carry herself. These were non-negotiable and he would never again bend on getting exactly what he wanted. He took this list and put it away in a drawer. The woman of his dreams showed up less than a month later. He met her at a business meeting that he didn't even want to attend. He followed the universe as it gnawed at him to go to this meeting. They have now been together for eight years. It never would have happened if Peter had not set his goal, Nevillized it and took inspired action. By doing this he was finally able to pick her out. This happens all the time!

As you go through your plan, you'll reach the goals you set. Then, you'll set new goals and strive toward them. So when do you know that you've finally made it? Hard to say. But when you do, take a deep breath and proclaim, "I've arrived!" This is different for every individual. Some have a particular benchmark. For some it's an amount of money. For others it may be a deadline. Then there are some who leave it open-ended and just follow their gut instinct. Every time I complete a big goal, I set an even higher one. You may find this true of you as well. Once you find something you love doing with passion, why would you ever stop?

I think you will reach an abundant, fulfilling life much sooner than you realize once you start on your path to success. Few realize that success isn't a thing – it's an emotion. We feel successful — therefore we are successful.

There are people perfectly content and happy working a mediocre job, raising their children and spending time with family. There is no rule saying you have to be dissatisfied with any of these elements of your life, or destitute on the streets, to pursue long-term financial goals. This is merely a starting point. You can always improve. The path to success isn't about getting to a final point. It's about the journey. What will you discover about yourself and others as you go? What lessons will you learn and want to share with those who may one day approach you and ask you to mentor them?

Journeying into an unknown territory is exciting and potentially frightening. It's this mixture of emotions that can confuse and distract you. Your mind will create fear as you strive toward your goal. If you let yourself dwell on that fear, it will manifest itself in reality.

You may have had the exhilaration and excitement of performing on stage. Even the most seasoned actor or singer can have butterflies in their stomach before the curtain rises or the lights go out. It's almost as if the mind is giving a final warning before you get on stage. It's no different when you're striving toward big goals. It's scary and exciting at the same time.

REACHING NEW HEIGHTS

As you reach new heights of awareness and success, you'll also find that your life needs balance. It's not just about money. Money isn't the main priority and never should be. There are other considerations like family, health and your own emotional well-being. Have you ever had a problem with your inner ear? If you have, then you know what it feels like to feel off balance. The world seems to spin and you become disoriented. Disorientation can feel exhilarating in the short-term. You never want to be out of balance. A well-balanced life involves both physical and emotional aspects. Living a well-balanced life means balancing your goals while taking time to enjoy the journey. If you want to live a fulfilling, meaningful life, you have to make adjustments and some tough choices.

It would be very easy to live a balanced life in an ideal world. What if you could sit down and write the story of your life, as you want to live it? What would you be like? What kind of possessions and finances would you have? What would make you happy? You have control over much of what will happen in your life. You're not a helpless puppet manipulated by people around you. You are able to make choices and decisions that will shape your future.

In the real world you're tasked with numerous demands on your time and resources. You may feel overwhelmed at times. When this occurs, you must make decisions about what you can and cannot do. These decisions are based on the goals you have, how you rank/prioritize these goals and how well you follow what you think is right for you.

Back in rougher days, I used to wonder if I had what it takes to be a success. Now I know I do. And so do you! I want you to stand in front of your mirror everyday and say aloud, "I have what it takes!"

Trust me – you do! Soon you'll know it too. Repeat the words "I have what it takes" over and over. Type them up and hang them on your refrigerator, wall or computer. Look at them each day and believe in yourself. Self-talk is powerful, but most of us talk ourselves down, not up. Be a cheerleader for yourself. Encourage yourself.

Embrace the changes in your life with a great, positive attitude. Read the Optimist Creed (at the front of this book) every day. Breathe it in. Commit to yourself that you will do whatever it takes to attain your goals and live the life you've always dreamed about.

Also, remember to stay patient. Change doesn't happen overnight and this will take time. Don't rush through your plan. You'll end up skipping steps and becoming frustrated. Remember that this is about the journey. You don't get to the top of the mountain in one day. You get there step-by-step with dogged persistence.

Take time to appreciate who you are today and who you want to become. Someday you'll look back and be proud of the decisions that you're making today, as well as the changes you're implementing.

Listen and think before you speak. A big part of learning is to be quiet and let others teach you. You never know what you may miss if you're talking instead of listening. Others may have valid input and they want to give it to you. Let them.

Don't fear change or uncertainty. Have faith in your ability to solve any problem that you'll encounter. Get the facts, do your homework and courageously move forward. Don't let "risk" keep you from the glorious rewards awaiting you.

Wealth is often hiding under what you fear to do. Face your fears and take inspired action. Dare something worthy – and begin it today. The result will be a new flow of money! *That's* how you attract money now!

THE FREEDOM TO LIVE! TRUTHS & TAKE-AWAYS

STEPS TO ATTRACTING MONEY INTO YOUR LIFE:
Step 1: Alter How You Think
Step 2: Give Without Expectation
Step 3: Prosperous Spending
Step 4: Ask for Help
Step 5: Nevillize Your Goals
Step 6: Think Like an Entrepreneur
Step 7: Help Your Community & Your World

ACTION STEPS

- Work on becoming a mental magnet for money by reading books, listening to audio recordings, attending events designed to help you think more powerfully and prosperously, and/or getting a Miracles Coach.
- Give money weekly to wherever you received inspiration.
- Buy things that excite you without going into debt.
- Pray for guidance and ask others for help.
- Imagine attracting money now and what it feels like to be wealthy.
- Listen for complaints and find ways to turn them into products or services.
- Volunteer to help a cause or person you believe in.

{AFTERWORD}
TAKE INSPIRED ACTION NOW!

CONGRATULATIONS! YOU NOW KNOW the seven steps to attract money now.

But now that you know them, what will you do next?

Answer: You do whatever you're inspired to do to begin the process of attracting money now. In other words, don't sit on your butt and wait for money to rain on you. Take inspired action RIGHT NOW.

Many people have the information on what to do and how to do it. The challenge is that they don't implement it. If you keep on doing what you've always done, you'll always have the results you have right now. Isn't it time for a big change? Isn't that time now? Don't you deserve the wealth and happiness you've been longing for?

Money is a powerful, positive tool. It's a vehicle for accomplishing great things. You can help yourself, your family, your friends, your community and the world. With money, you can buy fun toys for yourself. Admit it, you'd enjoy that. You'll also be able to make a difference in areas you care about. All you need is money. And now, with the seven-step formula I've revealed to you, you can attract money now.

I've done my part. I've written *Attract Money Now* and put all the tools in your hands. The next steps are yours. If you want personal help, consider my famous Miracles Coaching™ program. See www.miraclescoaching.com.

God speed to you.

With love,

Dr. Joe Vitale

{BONUS}
29 WAYS TO ATTRACT MONEY NOW

1. If you're in the United States and in need of help for an emergency service, call 211.

2. Call the USA Silent Unity prayer line: 1-740-362-4214.

3. Give money to wherever you received inspiration or encouragement.

4. Buy something you want and can afford.

5. Take action on an idea you have.

6. Write a script of you being wealthy and how it feels.

7. Watch the movie, *The Secret*. www.thesecret.tv

8. Watch the movie, *The Compass*. www.thecompass.tv

9. Watch the movie, *Try It On Everything*. www.tryitoneverything.com

10. Use *EFT* to help dissolve feelings of desperation. www.emofree.com

11. Turn off the mainstream news.

12. Join or create a support group, such as Attract Miracles Online. *www.attractmiracles.com*

13. Forgive yourself and others.

Bonus: 29 Ways to Attract Money Now

14. Read *Think and Grow Rich*.

15. Turn a problem into a product and sell it online.

16. Feel grateful for something you have.

17. Practice the seven steps in *Attract Money Now*.

18. Listen to *The Secret to Attracting Money*.

19. Get a Miracles Coach. www.miraclescoaching.com

20. Pray.

21. Create a vision board of what you want.

22. Do 5 things each day on items on your vision board.

23. Ask for help.

24. Help someone else.

25. Worship time, not money. Use your time wisely.

26. Imagine what you would do if you won the lotto for $37 million. Do it.

27. Do whatever you're afraid to do. Wealth is hiding behind your fear.

28. Get a job. While you pursue your dream, feed yourself with work.

29. Get clear of limiting beliefs about money using Morty Lefkoe's Belief Work *http://www.recreateyourlife.com* or *www.moneybeyondbelief.com*

{SUPER BONUS}
THE SECRET TO ATTRACT MONEY NOW! THE HOW: SETTING EFFECTIVE GOALS

You can have all the money you want as soon as you realize it's not needed to be happy."
— JOE VITALE

NOW THAT YOU HAVE asked yourself what you want, and investigated some possibilities for generating revenue, how do you go about it? It's the details that people get hung up on and can allow your fears to balloon to the point that you don't take any action at all. There's a great deal of trepidation about whether you should even try to attract money when the economy is in a slump. Of course you should. What better time is there? A down economy offers openings and opportunities that just don't exist when things are booming.

For example, Hyatt opened its first hotel at Los Angeles Airport (LAX) in the late 1950s. The US was going through a major recession at the time. Hyatt now has over 365 hotels in 25 countries. Burger King and IHOP also began during the same recession.

One of the major recessions that I experienced myself in the early 1970s spawned both Lexis-Nexis, the web-based research hub, and FedEx. The 2001 recession saw the debut of Wikipedia and Internet giants Google and PayPal. They thrived during this time. Don't allow the media's negativity or the opinions of others to convince you to wait for a better time. There is no better time other than now. And if you never start, you'll never reap the benefits.

In order to get from a vague idea of what you want to accomplish, you have to set clear goals, and then break those goals into doable steps. While this takes time to outline, it will keep you moving forward toward your goal and allow you to see when you get distracted or fall off the intended path. Some find goal setting a tedious process and it's powerful. It forces you to refine every nuance of what you're doing and where you're going. Each path is an active choice and clear goals make those choices easy. I also find goals to be motivating. You have to push yourself. And I know that without really strong goals I tend to slack off and do what's easy – rather than striving for more.

It intrigues me that almost every high achieving individual, whether an entrepreneur, CEO, or professional athlete, takes the time to make daily, weekly, monthly, yearly and multi-year goals. If all the people at the top are doing it, it makes sense that those wanting to attract money into their lives would do it without question. Still few of them do. There's no way to maintain your long-term vision as well as short-term motivation without setting and then tracking your goals.

By setting clear and well-defined goals, you can evaluate your progress and take pride in your accomplishments. You can confirm that you're making progress, though it might seem like you're not moving much. Achieving written goals also allows you to look back and see how far you've come.

SETTING EFFECTIVE GOALS

You may have an idea for a business and you may have an idea of what you want to accomplish with your additional revenue stream. And that's great! Until you have those ideas defined and organized, you won't have a clear direction.

There are good goals and not-so-good goals. There are certain elements that good goals have in common. Good goals are:

Clear and Specifically Defined - In order to be as effective as possible, your goals must be clearly defined. This means that instead of saying, "I want more money," you write "I want to attract an additional $500 per month within six months." You want something that you can really Nevillize and attach to emotionally. It's like watching a fuzzy video. You can't really get involved at this point as it is unclear. Technically, $10 is "more money" yet that amount likely will not really make a difference in your life. Always be specific and focus on that goal.

Achievable in a Given Time Frame – It's important that you put a deadline on your goals. Otherwise, they just remain wishes. 'Someday' is not a time frame! You want to set a deadline that is reasonable and challenging. A time frame with a deadline gives you self-imposed deadlines that move you forward, so you're consistently making progress. A goal without a deadline puts no pressure on you to accomplish it. There's also no way to measure your progress. For example, if you set a goal to run a marathon, but you don't choose a marathon to run in, or a date for its completion, why bother training for it?

Commitment to Steady Progress – This means discipline. That can really trip you up. You want to set small tasks each day that get you closer to your goal and then commit to doing that task. This is progress. If you decide you want to write a book but then don't commit to disciplined, steady progress, time passes and you still haven't completed the book. This is why you see someone at the family reunion who wanted to write a book 20 years ago, but is still 'working on it.' In fact, the problem is that they've never really committed to working on it. Don't kid yourself that you can set a goal, Nevillize it every day and make no progress. Accomplishment requires action – so don't let yourself off the hook. Start it, take inspired action and get it done.

Align your short and long-term goals – This is one I still constantly remind myself of. It's easy to get excited and say, "I want to write books, do seminars, be a speaker, travel, have an Internet business, and anything else." Having too many unfocused goals leads you in too many different directions, causing you to spread yourself too thin. You only have 24 hours each day, so you must focus on a few goals at a time, and then gradually add others. Be sure the daily tasks you undertake are working toward something and not just keeping you busy. For example, if you want to start an Internet business and run around meeting with graphic designers and consultants, but never really decide what product or service you are going to sell, then this is just busy work that isn't getting you anywhere. Decide what the goals are before you take inspired action or you will take part in meaningless activity that gets you nowhere.

Flexibility – Your goals have to be flexible. There will be times you completely underestimate the amount of time it takes to accomplish something. When that happens, you have to be able to decelerate the timeline and still make good progress. Conversely, there will be times you set a six-month goal and suddenly it gets done in six weeks! That is great! At these times you want to accelerate your goals. Keep pushing yourself.

Please never confuse goals and tasks. Goals are the big targets and tasks are the stepping stones to accomplishing your goals. For example, if your goal is to develop a set of workout DVDs, then checking out production costs quotes with three different companies may be a task. Doing small tasks toward your goal each day is important because it gives you a sense of control and accomplishment.

Also, be sure that all the small tasks are working toward the goal. It's easy to seem busy and not get anywhere. Write down each activity you perform and evaluate it on a weekly basis. You'll see if you're spending too much time on things that are not important.

PRIORITIZING YOUR GOALS

You are only one person, with big dreams and only so much time each day. How do you decide which goals are the most important and which ones should be put on hold? There is an effective, easy way to sort your goals and decide which ones go where on your priority list. Write a list of your top 30 goals. Yes, 30 is a lot for some people. But in order to get to the good ones, you have to write them all down.

Once you have 30, go through them and take out the 10 that are the least important. Set those aside and put them in Group 3. Now look at the 20 you have left and remove the 10 that are the next least important. They are Group 2. Now you're down to 10 goals – the ones you believe are the most important. These are Group 1 goals.

The way to prioritize these 10 is to take a few minutes, close your eyes and focus on each goal one-by-one. Which goal produces the biggest emotional connection? It goes first. Go down the list and rank them in the order of your emotional connection, with the deepest emotional connection at the top and the weakest at the bottom.

These are the 10 goals you should be working on. You may be glancing over at some of your Group 2 or Group 3 goals and be tempted to start on them. You're likely tempted, because they are easier or faster to accomplish. They would take away time that you need to accomplish tasks toward the goals most important to you.

Anytime you question which goal or project needs to take precedence, just stop for a few minutes and ask yourself which one has the strongest positive emotional connection. This will give you the answer. Then it's your responsibility to take inspired action on it.

LONG TERM AND SHORT TERM GOALS

Everyone needs both short and long-term goals. The long-term goals are your overall objectives and usually have a time line of five years or more. Short-term goals align with those long-term goals – meaning that they play a part in getting to that big overall goal but they have a much shorter time line. Usually six months to a year. Tasks are the weekly or daily steps you take to accomplish your short-term goals.

You may be wondering, "Why not just make the big long-term goals and do away with all these short-term goals?" Individuals perform better with regular and consistent reinforcement. As you track your progress, and see how many short-term goals you've accomplished, it makes the long-term goals seem that much closer and easier to reach.

Long-term goals have a very important function as well. In addition to giving you an overall direction, they also provide a focal point when times get hard or you suffer setbacks. Focusing on the long-term goal and being able to see the big picture, can get you through those times when it would be easy to quit. It allows you to see your situation as temporary and gives you the will to search for solutions. As you overcome each difficulty it builds the confidence you'll need to push on toward that long-term goal.

Now comes the fun part. You get to put the short and long-term goals together to get the best results. Let me give you a couple of examples to illustrate this.

MARK – THE MATH TEACHER

Mark teaches math at a local high school. Eventually he wants to create a home-based learning system for kids that will improve their math skills. He wants to earn more money and become financially free so he can quit his regular teaching job and tutor those kids who need help. When Mark imagines these goals, he has the most emotional connection to financial freedom. So for Mark, his goals might look like this:

Long-term Goal: Replace income and quit job.
  A. **Short-term Goals Related to Long-Term Goal**
   1. Start Tutoring
   2. Create Math Home Study Courses
 1. **Weekly tasks related to short-term goal**
   1. Post notices on school billboards advertising math tutoring services

2. Speak with teachers and school counselors one-on-one and let them know Mark is offering math tutoring
2. **Weekly tasks related to short-term goal**
1. Define age groups that will benefit from home study
2. List content for curriculum

You can see how the long-term and short-term goals are interrelated. They're not separate but support each other. Now let's look at another example.

LYDIA – THE YOGA INSTRUCTOR

Lydia has a successful yoga studio. She feels she has a winning formula that can be resold as a franchise and duplicated across the country. Lydia wants to increase her public profile and position herself as an expert, so she can increase the value of her brand as well as the franchise.

Long-term Goal: Have a national franchise of yoga studios across the country.
  A. **Short-term Goals Related to Long-term Goal**
    1. Write a book positioning Lydia as a yoga expert
    2. Create beginner, intermediate and advanced DVDs to sell via infomercials, allowing her to make her yoga brand a household name
  1. **Weekly tasks related to the short-term goal**
    1. Consult with a writer and organize information into an outline
    2. Set aside a minimum of 45 minutes a day, three times per week to create content
  2. **Weekly tasks related to the short-term goal**
    1. Investigate production costs for DVDs
    2. Determine the applicable routines to produce for the beginner DVD

People spend hours, days and even weeks getting hung up on trying to figure out how to get started achieving their dreams. It's really logical. If you use the information in this chapter, you'll have a very easy, workable plan without hours or days of tedious indecision. Decide what you need to do and then start doing it.

I find the goal setting process to be very motivating. In order to sustain that motivation, you have to select goals that are within your realm of control and a realistic timetable. What does this mean? Let's say you decide that you want to make a million dollars and have your own reality show within a year. While you may be able to accomplish both of these goals in the long term – attempting to complete them within a year may be unrealistic. You have to have certain skills to accomplish both of these goals.

Just like it's unrealistic to think you can lose 50 pounds in a month and keep it off over the long term – it's also unrealistic to think you can make one million dollars in a year in an Internet business without any experience. You have to put in the time and effort to learn the business and it will pay off for you in the end.

Planning and thinking about your goals is never a waste of your time. After all, knowing what not to do is almost as important as knowing what to do. By doing your homework, and learning from experienced mentors, you'll avoid the pitfalls and mistakes of others. Every setback you avoid is time saved toward achieving your long-term goal.

Many obstacles may get in your way as you strive to reach your goals. That's called Life. But by studying where you want to go and how you're going to get there, you'll have a clear path which will help you avoid problems.

The flip side of setting unrealistic goals is to set goals that are too low. Something that is easily attainable, but does not qualify as a goal. Don't underestimate yourself or discount your skills. You'll become bored with a goal too easy to reach. You'll lose interest. You need something that engages you and challenges you.

Pick goals that challenge you professionally, mentally and even spiritually. Go for ideas that make you stretch your possibilities and require a high level of creativity and energy. You'll never achieve great things without pushing yourself. Goals that don't push you, move you sideways, not forward. They don't get you out of your comfort zone or force you to learn new and difficult lessons. It takes two key factors to reach any goal, seriousness and flexibility.

Being serious about a goal means that you take the necessary steps, whatever those may be, to achieve it. You're giving yourself self-imposed deadlines for specific tasks and evaluating your own progress. Then you develop the next set of strategic tasks to move forward. The first step, if you're serious, is to write down your goal. The second step is to announce it publicly. This may seem like you're giving those around you the opportunity to ridicule you in advance. And some may. By first writing your goal down and then announcing it, it provides additional motivation, since you know people will be asking about your progress. This gives you accountability to yourself, as well as others.

You've probably heard people close to you announce their plans. How did they do it? Did they say, "I'm going to lose 50 pounds and run a 10K by this time next year," or did they say something like, "After the holidays I'm going to lose weight and then I'll be able to do what I want"?

If you heard someone make the first statement, you would assume they're serious and committed to their goals. However, if you heard the second statement, you'd wonder how serious they were, or if this is just a hope of theirs that they don't really plan to work toward. This person, instead of setting a goal and being willing to work hard to get what they want, is content to just wish and get nowhere. Procrastination is not your friend. If you're thinking that you will start working toward your goals after the holidays, on your birthday, or after such and such happens, you are just deluding yourself. Every day you wait is a day wasted. You don't get it back and you don't get to try again. The day is gone forever. So get busy!

The second key factor to reaching your goal is flexibility. This does not mean giving yourself a break and being lazy. This means using creativity to overcome obstacles and listening to feedback. This will help you fine tune your goals as you go. You must have the ability to step back on a regular basis (I recommend at least monthly) and evaluate your progress. What worked? What didn't? What changes are you going to make in your strategy and task list next month?

Goal planning involves risk. That could mean risking a wrong move, bad decision or even a major setback. It also means that you must be adaptable to changing circumstances. You must still juggle work, family and bills in addition to striving toward your long-term goals. There are times when certain goals will take a backseat to others, but all of these instances give you the opportunity to be creative, and perhaps even come up with another opportunity that fits into your long-term goals.

Feedback is important because no matter how well you've researched or planned, there may be some areas that you've overlooked or are unaware of. You may also lose your perspective from time to time and be unable to correctly assess your own efforts. At those times a wise or experienced friend or family member can help you get back on track.

Mentors and mastermind partners who are aware of your goals will also be able to offer encouragement. Talk to them about where you are on the path to your goals, what progress you've made and what problems you've encountered. They may be able to offer you some good suggestions or solutions. And always consider using a coach, maybe one from my own Miracles Coaching™ program.

There are times when you have doubts and these can be compounded by family and friends who may be telling you everything you can't do and discouraging you from moving forward. You have to remember to focus on your plan. This means not letting negative emotions get the best of you to the point you 'try to prove everyone wrong.' While harsh comments may motivate you to strive toward your goal, they may also lead you into the pit of self-sabotage. When you allow others to affect your plan, you may try to accelerate it to prove something. You can end up with less than you started.

You must guard yourself against this kind of reaction. Stick to your plan and avoid the traps. Keep your avenues open to receiving everything available. Build on what you have. Learn from each lesson as you make consistent progress. One of Newton's laws of physics is that 'An object in motion stays in motion, while an object at rest stays at rest.' The same is true for the human mind. If you feel in control and like you're making progress, then it is easier to keep going. However, if you feel out of control and come to a stop, then it takes even more effort to get going again.

Nobody navigates this perfectly. That's okay. You don't need to be perfect, just committed to having an open heart to receive and you'll be given what you need to make your dreams comes true. Keep your awareness open so you can see the changes you need to make and take inspired action to make them. Wealthy people know that goals can be changed as new information comes in. Be flexible while keeping your eye on the prize.

Remember, the super bonus secret to attract money now is to have goals that inspire you and thrill you.

{BONUS}
A DIVINE WAY TO CLEAR LIMITING BELIEFS ABOUT MONEY

MANY YEARS AGO, I heard about a therapist in Hawaii who helped cure a complete ward of criminally insane patients--without ever seeing any of them. The psychologist would study an inmate's chart and then look within himself to see how he created that person's illness. As he improved himself, the patient improved.

When I first heard this story, I thought it was an urban legend. How could anyone heal anyone else by healing himself? How could even the best self-improvement master cure the criminally insane?

It didn't make any sense. It wasn't logical, so I dismissed the story.

However, I heard it again a year later. I heard that the therapist had used a Hawaiian healing process called ho'oponopono. I had never heard of it, yet I couldn't let it leave my mind. If the story was at all true, I had to know more.

I had always understood "total responsibility" to mean that I am responsible for what I think and do. Beyond that, it's out of my hands. I think that most people think of total responsibility that way. We're responsible for what we do, not what anyone else does. The Hawaiian therapist who healed those mentally ill people would teach me an advanced new perspective about total responsibility.

His name is Dr. Ihaleakala Hew Len. We probably spent an hour talking on our first phone call. I asked him to tell me the complete story of his work as a therapist. He explained that he worked at Hawaii State Hospital for four years. That ward where they kept the criminally insane was dangerous. Psychologists quit on a monthly basis. The staff called in sick a lot or simply quit. People would walk through that ward with their backs against the wall, afraid of being attacked by patients. It was not a pleasant place to live, work, or visit.

Dr. Hew Len told me that he never saw patients. He agreed to have an office and to review their files. While he looked at those files, he would work on himself. As he worked on himself, patients began to heal.

"After a few months, patients that had to be shackled were being allowed to walk freely," he told me. "Others who had to be heavily medicated were getting off their medications. And those who had no chance of ever being released were being freed."

I was in awe.

"Not only that," he went on, "but the staff began to enjoy coming to work. Absenteeism and turnover disappeared. We ended up with more staff than we needed because patients were being released, and all the staff was showing up to work. Today, that ward is closed."

This is where I had to ask the million dollar question: "What were you doing within yourself that caused those people to change?"

"I was simply healing the part of me that created them," he said.

I didn't understand.

Dr. Hew Len explained that total responsibility for your life means that everything in your life – simply because it is in your life – is your responsibility. In a literal sense the entire world is your creation.

Whew. This is tough to swallow. Being responsible for what I say or do is one thing. Being responsible for what everyone in my life says or does is quite another. Yet, the truth is this: if you take complete responsibility for your life, then everything you see, hear, taste, touch, or in any way experience is your responsibility because it is in your life.

This means that terrorist activity, the president, the economy, and your own financial situation – anything you experience and don't like – is up for you to heal. They don't exist, in a manner of speaking, except as projections from inside you. The problem isn't with them, it's with you, and to change them, you have to change you.

I know this is tough to grasp, let alone accept or actually live. Blame is far easier than total responsibility, but as I spoke with Dr. Hew Len, I began to realize that healing for him and in ho'oponopono means loving yourself. If you want to improve your life, you have to heal your life. If you want to cure anyone--even a mentally ill criminal--you do it by healing you.

This also goes for your money situation. If you want to clear your beliefs about money and begin to attract money now, you have to address the issue within yourself.

I asked Dr. Hew Len how he went about healing himself. What

A Divine Way to Clear Limiting Beliefs About Money

was he doing, exactly, when he looked at those patients' files?

"I just kept saying, 'I'm sorry' and 'I love you,' over and over again," he explained.

That's it?

That's it.

Turns out that loving yourself is the greatest way you improve yourself, and as you improve yourself, you improve your world.

Let me give you a quick example of how this works: one day, someone sent me an email that upset me. In the past I would have handled it by working on my emotional hot buttons or by trying to reason with the person who sent the nasty message. This time, I decided to try Dr. Hew Len's method. I kept silently saying, "I'm sorry" and "I love you." I didn't say it to anyone in particular. I was simply evoking the spirit of love to heal within me what was creating the outer circumstance.

Within an hour I got an e-mail from the same person. He apologized for his previous message. Keep in mind that I didn't take any outward action to get that apology. I didn't even write him back. Yet, by saying "I love you," I somehow healed within me what was creating him.

I later attended a ho'oponopono workshop run by Dr. Hew Len. He's now 70 years old, considered a grandfatherly shaman, and is somewhat reclusive. He praised my book, *The Attractor Factor*. He told me that as I improve myself, my book's vibration will raise, and everyone will feel it when they read it. In short, as I improve, my readers will improve.

"What about the books that are already sold and out there?" I asked.

"They aren't out there," he explained, once again blowing my mind with his mystic wisdom. "They are still in you."

In short, there is no out there.

It would take a whole book to explain this advanced technique with the depth it deserves (which is why Dr. Hew Len and I wrote the book *Zero Limits*). Suffice it to say that whenever you want to improve anything in your life, there's only one place to look: inside you.

"When you look, do it with love."

BIBLIOGRAPHY

If you want to be wealthier, healthier and happier, you must continue to learn and grow. Here are many great books (and a few audio recordings) to help you along your path to freedom. Your library or local bookstore or Amazon.com will have these.

Allen, James. *As A Man Thinketh.*

Assaraf, John. *The Answer.* Atria, 2008.

Atkinson, William Walter. *Thought Vibration, or The Law of Attraction in the Thought World.* Chicago: New Thought Publishing, 1906.

Ball, Ron, et al. *Freedom at Your Fingertips.* Fredericksburg, VA: In Roads Publishing, 2006.

Barrett, Rick, and Vitale, Joe. *Give to Live.* www.givetolivebook.com 2008.

Beckwith, Michael Bernard. *Spiritual Liberation.*

Behrend, Genevieve, and Vitale, Joe. *How to Attain Your Desires by Letting Your Subconscious Mind Work for You, Vol.1.* Garden City, NY: Morgan-James Publishing, 2004.

Behrend, Genevieve, and Vitale, Joe. *How to Attain Your Desires, Vol 2: How to Live Life and Love It!* GardenCity, NY: Morgan-James Publishing, 2005.

Bender, Sheila Sidney, and Sise, Mary. *The Energy of Belief: Psychology's Power Tools to Focus Intention and Release Blocking Beliefs.* Santa Rosa, CA: Energy Psychology Press, 2008.

Bowen, Will. *A Complaint Free World.* New York: Doubleday, 2007.

Braden, Gregg. *The Divine Matrix: Bridging Time, Space, Miracles, and Belief.* Carlsbad, CA: Hay House, 2006.

Bristol, Claude. *The Magic of Believing.* New York: Pocket Books, 1991.

Bruce, Alexandra. *Beyond the Secret.* New York: Disinformation Company, 2007.

Bibliography

Butterworth, Eric. *Spiritual Economics: The Principles and Process of True Prosperity*. Lee's Summit, MO: Unity, 1993.

Byrne, Rhonda. *The Secret*. New York: Atria Books/Beyond Words, 2006.

Callahan, Roger. *Tapping the Healer Within: Using Thought-Field Therapy to Instantly Conquer Your Fears, Anxieties, and Emotional Distress*. New York: McGraw-Hill, 2002.

Canfield, Jack, and Switzer, Janet. *The Success Principles: How to Get from Where You Are to Where You Want to Be*. New York: Collins, 2006.

Casey, Karen. *Change Your Mind and Your Life Will Follow*. New York: Conari Press, 2005.

Chopra, Deepak. *The Spontaneous Fulfillment of Desire*. New York: Harmony, 2003.

Coates, Denise. *Feel It Real! The Magical Power of Emotions*. Place unknown: Denise Coates Publishers, 2006.

Coppel, Paula Godwin. *Sacred Secrets: Finding Your Way to Joy, Peace and Prosperity*. Unity Village, MO: 2008.

Cornyn-Selby, Alyce. *What's Your Sabotage?* Portland, OR: Beynch Press, 2000.

Craig, K.C. *Placing Your Order: Steps for Successful Manifestations*. Fairfax, VA: RMS Publications, 2007.

Dahl, Lynda Madden. *Beyond the Winning Streak: Using Conscious Creation to Consistently Win at Life*. Woodbridge Group, 2000.

Dahl, Lynda Madden. *Ten Thousand Whispers: A Guide to Conscious Creation*. Woodbridge Group, 1995.

Dahl, Lynda Madden. *The Wizards of Consciousness: Making the Imponderable Practical*. Woodbridge Group, 1997.

Deutschman, Alan. *Change or Die: The Three Keys to Change at Work and in Life*. New York: Reagan Books, 2007.

DiMarsico, Bruce. *The Option Method: Unlock Your Happiness with Five Simple Questions*. Walnut Grove, CA: Dragonfly Press, 2006.

Dore, Carole. *The Emergency Handbook for Getting Money Fast!* San Francisco: Celestial Arts, 2002.

Doyle, Bob. *Wealth Beyond Reason*. Duluth, GA: Boundless Living, 2004.

Dwoskin, Hale. *The Sedona Method: Your Key to Lasting Happiness, Success, Peace and Emotional Well-Being*. Sedona, AZ: Sedona Press, 2003.

Dyer, Wayne. *The Power of Intention: Learning to Co-Create Your World Your Way*. Carlsbad, CA: Hay House, 2004.

Eker, T. Harv. *Secrets of the Millionaire Mind: Mastering the Inner Game of Wealth.* NY: Collins, 2005.

Ellsworth, Paul. *Mind Magnet: How to Unify and Intensify Your Natural Faculties for Efficiency, Health and Success.* Holyoke, MA: Elizabeth Towne Company, 1924.

Evans, Mandy. *Traveling Free: How to Recover from the Past.* Encinitas, CA: Yes You Can Press, 2005.

Fengler, Fred, and Varnum, Todd. *Manifesting Your Heart's Desires, Book I and Book II.* Burlington, VT: Heart Light, 2002.

Ferguson, Bill. *Heal the Hurt that Sabotages Your Life.* Houston, TX: Return to the Heart, 2004.

Fisher, Donna. *Power Networking.*

Fisher, Mark. *The Instant Millionaire: A Tale of Wisdom and Wealth.* New World Library, 1993.

Ford, Debbie. *The Dark Side of the Light Chasers.* New York: River Head Books, 1998.

Ford, Debbie. *Why Good People Do Bad Things: How to Stop Being Your Own Worst Enemy.* New York: Harper One, 2008.

Furnham, Adrian. *The Psychology of Money.*

Gage, Randy. *Why You're Dumb, Sick & Broke… And How to Get Smart, Healthy & Rich!* Hoboken, NJ: John Wiley & Sons, 2006.

Gaines, Edwene. *The Four Spiritual Laws of Prosperity.* Pa: Rodale Press, 2005.

Gillett, Dr. Richard. *Change Your Mind, Change Your World.* New York: Simon & Schuster, 1992.

Gilmore, Ehryck. *The Law of Attraction 101.* Chicago: Eromlig Publishing, 2006.

Goi, James. *How to Attract Money Using Mind Power.* West Conshohocken, PA: Infinity Publishing, 2007.

Goldberg, Bruce. *Karmic Capitalism: A Spiritual Approach to Financial Independence.* Baltimore, MD: Publish America, 2005.

Grabhorn, Lynn. *Excuse Me, Your Life is Waiting: The Astonishing Power of Feelings.* Charlottsville, VA: Hampton Roads, 2003.

Gregory, Eva. *The Feel Good Guide to Prosperity.* San Francisco: Life Coaching, 2005.

Hall, Philip. *Jesus Taught It, Too: The Early Roots of the Law of Attraction.* Alberta, Canada: Avatar, 2007.

Hartong, Leo. *Awakening to the Dream.*

Hamilton, Roger. *Your Life, Your Legacy.*

Bibliography

Harris, Bill. *Thresholds of the Mind: Your Personal Road map to Success, Happiness, and Contentment.* Beaverton, OR: Centerpoint Research, 2002.

Hawkins, David. *Devotional Nonduality.* Sedona, AZ: Veritas Publishing, 2006.

Hawkins, David. *Healing and Recovery.* Sedona, AZ: Veritas Publishing, 2009.

Hawkins, David. *I: Reality and Subjectivity.* Sedona, AZ: Veritas Publishing, 2003.

Hawkins, David. *Transcending the Levels of Consciousness.* Sedona, AZ: Veritas Publishing, 2006.

Hawkins, David. *Power vs. Force: The Hidden Determinants of Human Behavior.* Carlsbad, CA: Hay House, 2002.

Helmstetter, Shad. *Self-Talk Solution.* New York: Pocket Books, 1987.

Helmstetter, Shad. *What to Say When You Talk to Yourself.* New York: Pocket Books, 1982.

Hicks, Jerry and Esther. *Ask and It Is Given: Learning to Manifest Your Desires.* Carlsbad, CA: Hay House, 2004.

Hicks, Jerry and Esther. *The Law of Attraction: the Basics of the Teachings of Abraham.* Carlsbad, CA: Hay House, 2006.

Hicks, Jerry and Esther. *Money and the Law of Attraction.*

Hill, Napoleon. *Think and Grow Rich.*

Holmes, Ernest. *Creative Mind and Success.* San Francisco: Tarcher, 2004.

Holmes, Ernest. *Science of Mind.* San Francisco: Tarcher, 1998.

Houlder, Kulananda and Dominic. *Mindfulness and Money.* New York: Broadway, 2002.

Kahler, Rick and Fox, Kathleen. *Conscious Finance: Uncover Your Hidden Money Beliefs and Transform the Role of Money in Your Life.* Rapid City, SD: Fox Craft: 2005.

Kaufman, Barry Neil. *To Love Is to Be Happy With.* New York: Fawcett, 1985.

Kennedy, Dan. *No B.S. Marketing to the Affluent.* (Foreword by Joe Vitale)

Kennedy, Dan. *No B.S. Wealth Attraction for Entrepreneurs.* Entrepreneur Press, 2006.

Kramer, Carolyn Miller. *Creating Miracles: Understanding the Experience of Divine Intervention.* Tiboron, CA: 1995.

Katie, Bryon. *Loving What Is. Four Questions that Can Change Your Life.*

Landrum, Gene. *The Superman Syndrome: The Magic of Myth in the Pursuit of Power: the Positive Mental Moxie of Myth for Personal Growth.* iUniverse, 2005.

Lapin, Jackie. *The Art of Conscious Creation.* Charleston, SC: Elevate, 2007.

Lapin, Rabbi Daniel. *Thou Shall Prosper: Ten Commandments for Making Money.* Hoboken, NJ: J Wiley & Sons, 2002.

Larson, Christian D. *Your Forces and How to Use Them.* London. Fowler, 1912.

Larson, Melody. *The Beginner's Guide to Abundance.* Booklocker.com, 2007.

Laut, Phil. *Money Is My Friend.*

Lefkoe, Morty. *Re-Create your Life.*

Levenson, Lester. *The Ultimate Truth About Love & Happiness: A Handbook for Life.* Sherman Oaks, CA: Lawrence Crane Enterprises, 2003.

Lichtman, Stuart, and Vitale, Joe. *How to Get Lots of Money for Anything FAST.* E-book, 2002.

Lipton, Bruce. *The Biology of Belief: Unleashing the Power of Consciousness, Matter and Miracles.* Mountain of Love, 2005.

Losier, Michael. *Law of Attraction.* Victoria, Canada: Losier Publications 2003.

Love, Lisa. *Beyond the Secret: Spiritual Power and the Law of Attraction.* Charlottesville, VA: Hampton Roads, 2007.

Mackenzie, Kathleen. *Not Manifesting? This Book is for You!* Denver, CO: Outskirts Press, 2007.

Martin, Art. *Your Body is Talking, Are You Listening?* Penryn, CA: Personal Transformation, 2001.

McCormick, Paul. *Secrets of the Millionaire Inside.*

McTaggart, Lynne. *The Intention Experiment: Using Your Thoughts to Change Your Life and the World.* New York: Free Press, 2007.

Miller, Scott. *Until It's Gone.*

Murphy, Dr. Joseph. *How to Attract Money.*

Murphy, Dr. Joseph. *The Power of Your Subconscious Mind.* New York: Bantam 2001.

Neville, Goddard, and Vitale, Joe. *At Your Command.* Garden City, NY: Morgan-James Publishing 2005.

Neville, Goddard. *Immortal Man: A Compilation of Lectures.* Camarillo, CA: DeVorss & Company, 1984.

Norville, Deborah. *Thank You Power: Making the Science of Gratitude Work for You.* Nashville, TN: Thomas Nelson, 2007.

Oates, Robert. *Permanent Peace: How to Stop Terrorism and War—Now and*

Bibliography

Forever. Fairfield, VA: Oates, 2002.

O'Bryan, Pat, and Vitale, Joe. *The Myth of Passive Income: The Problem and the Solution.* E-book, 2004. www.mythofpassiveincome.com

O'Bryan, Pat, and Vitale, Joe. *The Think and Grow Rich Workbook* is a free e-book based on the classic by Napoleon Hill. E-book, 2004. www.InstantChange.com

Patterson, Kerry. *Influencers: The Power to Change Anything.* New York: McGraw-Hill, 2008.

Pauley, Tom. *I'm Rich Beyond My Wildest Dreams, I Am, I Am, I Am.* New York: Rich Dreams, 1999.

Pavlina, Steve. *Personal Improvement for Smart People.*

Pilzer, Paul Zane. *God Wants You To Be Rich.*

Ponder, Catherine. *The Dynamic Laws of Prosperity.* Amarillo, TX: DeVorss, 1985.

Proctor, Bob. *It's Not About the Money.* Burman Books, 2008.

Proctor, Bob. *You Were Born Rich: Now You Can Discover and Develop Those Riches.* Toronto, Canada: Life Success Productions, 1997.

Rahula, Bhikkhu Basnagoda. *The Buddha's Teachings on Prosperity.*

Rafter, Mark. *The Wealth Manifesto: Transforming Your Life from Survive to Thrive.* Auburn, CA: New Knowledge Press, 2008.

Ray, James Arthur. *Harmonic Wealth.* Hyperion, 2008.

Ray, James Arthur. *The Science of Success: How to Attract Prosperity and Create Harmonic Wealth through Proven Principles.* Sun Ark Press, 1999.

Ressler, Peter, and Mitchell, Monika. *Spiritual Capitalism: How 9/11 Gave Us Nine Spiritual Lessons of Work and Business.* New York: Chilmark Books, 2007.

Rhinehart, Luke. *The Book of est.* www.bookofest.com

Ritt, Michael and Landers, Kirk. *A Lifetime of Riches: The Biography of Napoleon Hill.* New York: Dutton, 1995.

Roazzi, Vincent. *Spirituality of Success: Getting Rich with Integrity.* Dallas, TX: Namaste, 2001.

Roberts Jane. *The Nature of Personal Reality: Specific, Practical Techniques for Solving Everyday Problems and Enriching the Life You Know.* CA: New World Library, 1994.

Roman, Sanaya. *Creating Money: Attracting Abundance.*

Ross, Percy. *Ask for the Moon – and Get It!*

Rutherford, Darel. *So, Why Aren't You Rich?* Albuquerque, NM: Dar, 1998.

Ryce, Michael. *Why Is This Happening to Me—Again?* Theodosia, MO: Ryce, 1996.

Sage, Carnelian. *The Greatest Manifestation Principle in the World.* Beverley Hills, CA: Think Outside the Book, 2007.

Scheinfeld, Robert. *Busting Loose From The Money Game: Mind-Blowing Strategies for Changing the Rules of a Game You Can't Win.* Hoboken, NJ: John Wiley & Sons, 2006.

Shimoff, Marci. *Happy for No Reason.*

Shumsky, Susan. *Miracle Prayer: Nine Steps to Creating Prayers that Get Results.* Berkeley, CA: Celestial Arts, 2006.

Siebold, Steve. *177 Mental Toughness Secrets of the World Class.*

Staples, Dr. Walter Doyle. *Think Like A Winner!* Hollywood, CA: Wilshire, 1993.

Tipping, Colin. *Radical Manifestation: The Fine Art of Creating the Life You Want.* Marietta, GA: Global 13 Publications, 2006.

Trudeau, Kevin. *Debt Cures They Don't Want You To Know About.*

Truman, Karol. *Feelings Buried Alive Never Die...* Olympus, UT: 1991.

Trump, Donald. *Think BIG.*

Twist, Lynne. *The Soul of Money.*

Vitale, Joe. *Adventures Within: Confessions of an Inner World Journalist.* Author House, 2003.

Vitale, Joe. *Attract Money Now*, 2010.

Vitale, Joe. *The Attractor Factor: Five Easy Steps for Creating Wealth (or anything else) from the Inside Out.* Hoboken, NJ: John Wiley & Sons, 2005. Revised, 2008.

Vitale, Joe, and Ryan, Mark. *Attracting Wealth: Magnetizing Your Unconscious Mind for Prosperity: Subliminal Manifestation DVD #4.* Austin, TX: Hypnotic I Media, Inc., 2007. www.subliminalmanifestation.com

Vitale, Joe. *The Awakening Course.* Audio program. Hypnotic Marketing, Inc: Texas. 2008. www.awakeningdownload.com

Vitale, Joe. *Buying Trances: A New Psychology of Sales and Marketing.* Hoboken, NJ: John Wiley & Sons, 2007.

Vitale, Joe. *Expect Miracles.* Toronto, Canada. Burmam Books, 2008.

Vitale, Joe. *Hypnotic Writing.* Hoboken, NJ: John Wiley & Sons, 2007.

Vitale, Joe, with Perrine, Craig. *Inspired Marketing.*

Vitale, Joe. *Life's Missing Instruction Manual: the Guidebook You Should Have Been Given at Birth.* Hoboken, NJ: John Wiley & Sons, 2006.

Bibliography

Vitale, Joe. *The Greatest Money-Making Secret in History.* 1st Books Library, 2003.

Vitale, Joe. *The Key: The Missing Secret to Attracting Whatever You Want.* Hoboken, NJ: John Wiley & Sons, 2007.

Vitale, Joe and Hibbler, Bill. *Meet and Grow Rich.*

Vitale, Joe. *The Missing Secret: How to Use the Law of Attraction to Get Whatever You Want, Every Time.* Audio program. Niles, IL: Nightingale-Conant, 2008.

Vitale, Joe. *The Power of Outrageous Marketing!* Audio program. Niles, IL: Nightingale-Conant, 1998.

Vitale, Joe. *The Secret to Attracting Money.* Audio program. Niles, IL: Nightingale-Conant, 2009.

Vitale, Joe. *The Seven Lost Secrets of Success.* Hoboken, NJ: John Wiley & Sons, 2007.

Vitale, Joe. *There's a Customer Born Every Minute: P.T. Barnum's Amazing 10 "Rings of Power" for Creating Fame, Fortune, and a Business Empire Today—Guaranteed!* Hoboken, NJ: John Wiley & Sons, 2006.

Vitale, Joe, and Len, Ihaleakala Hew. *Zero Limits: The Secret Hawaiian System for Wealth, Health, Peace, and More.* Hoboken, NJ: John Wiley & Sons, 2007.

Waldroop, James, and Butler, Timothy. *The 12 Bad Habits that Hold Good People Back.* New York: Random House, 2000.

Wattles, Wallace D. *How to Get What You Want.* Publisher unknown.

Wattles, Wallace D. *The Science of Getting Rich.* New York: Penquin/Tarcher, 2007.

Wilde, Stuart. *The Trick to Money is Having Some.* Carlsbad, CA: Hay House, 1995.

Wojton, Djuna. *Karmic Healing: Clearing Past-Life Blocks to Present-Day Love, Health and Happiness.* Berkeley, CA: Crossing Press, 2006.

Wright, Kurt. *Breaking the Rules.* Boise, ID: CPM, 1998.

{RESOURCES}
GET HELP NOW

AHA! PROCESS
www.ahaprocess.com
Resources on the hidden rules of class and how to get ahead once you know them.

CAREER DEVELOPMENT AND JOB HUNTING
http://www.jobhuntersbible.com
Supplemental Internet site for the famous book, *What Color is Your Parachute?*

CONTINUUMS OF CARE (+ *COUNTY OR AREA*)
Google the "Continuums of Care Albuquerque" (type in your town, city, location, etc.).

These organizations coordinate federal & state funds related to homelessness & homeless prevention (like the homeless-related stimulus funds) and are mandated to coordinate the private & faith-based service providers in their catchment areas.

"FIRST CALL FOR HELP"
Dial 211 to get information in your area for immediate assistance.

"First Call For Help offers both confidential telephone support to people in crisis and personalized information and referrals to those needing assistance or wishing to contribute to their community."

Note: If 211 is not activated in your area, then dial 911 and ask for the local homeless shelter, job center, and/or counseling center.

GETTING AHEAD
http://www.gettingaheadnetwork.com/
Getting Ahead is an effective program to help people develop plans out of poverty and understand the hidden rules of the different economic

"classes." To see if there is one in your community or how to get one started, go to this link.

GOODWILL INDUSTRIES
http://locator.goodwill.org
Job preparation and placement help.

GOVERNMENT JOBS
http://www.usajobs.gov
Search for government jobs near you.

GOVERNMENT SITE (HUD)
www.hud.gov/foreclosure/index.cfm
Whether you're in foreclosure now or worried about it in the future, we have information that can help.

GOVERNMENT SPONSORED
www.hopenow.com
HOPE NOW is an alliance between HUD approved counseling agents, mortgage companies, investors and other mortgage market participants that provides free foreclosure prevention assistance.

HOMELESS COALITION (+ AREA)
The best way to access services in any area is to Google the "Homeless Coalition Albuquerque" (type in your town, city, location, etc.).

HOW TO GET A JOB
http://careerplanning.about.com/od/jobsearch/a/ref_get_a_job.htm
Great resource on how to get a job including resumes, interviews and personal marketing strategies.

MOVE THE MOUNTAIN
www.movethemountain.org
Nonprofit since 1992 committed to inspiring and equipping communities to end poverty.

NATIONAL COALITION FOR THE HOMELESS (NCH)
http://www.nationalhomeless.org/
Nation-wide programs, e.g., the *Faces of Homelessness* campaign that NCH VISTA volunteers are helping with.

OPERATION Y.E.S.
www.OperationYes.com
Your Economic Solution, prevent foreclosures and stop homelessness in America.

PERSONAL FINANCIAL MANAGEMENT SITE WITH A SENSE OF HUMOR
http://www.fool.com/personal-finance/index.aspx

THE INTERNATIONAL ASSOCIATION OF HOME BUSINESS OPPORTUNITIES
http://iaohbo.com/
The International Association of Home Business Opportunities is your "one-stop shopping" source for information on home business opportunities. Site gives members access to hundreds of legitimate home businesses from every area of the industry.

UNITED WAY
www.liveunited.org
Find your local united way and ask for programs that help people develop sustainable wages.

FOOD POWERS
http://www.foodpowers.com/joe_vitale.html

CATALOG OF PRODUCTS

BY DR. JOE VITALE

ATTRACT MONEY *NOW!*

"Give me 4 hours and I'll show you how to ATTRACT A NEW CAR (or anything else you can imagine) using my GUARANTEED 5-step easy system! I've attracted 7 new cars so far and now I'm teaching others how to manifest them! Want to be next?"

Would you like a brand new car despite your credit, your work status, or the amount of money you have in the bank?

Would you like to practically MAGICALLY MANIFEST IT?

Recently, 1,000 people called in from all over the world to listen to an unusual four-part tele-seminar series I hosted called *How to Attract a New Car*.

And the results were amazing. (Now **you will have the opportunity to listen in** on this riveting set of tele-seminars yourself.)

You have to stop and wonder…

- How can everyday average people like you and me actually attract new cars?
- How can a person get a Bentley (worth $250,000.00) for only $5,000?
- How can someone with no credit and no cash drive off with a brand new car?
- How can someone terrified of cars and car salesmen get over it in just days?
- How can I go from poverty to having BMW build a new car for me?
- How is all this possible?

Find out for yourself!

To learn more and order today, go to…

www.attractanewcar.com

What stage of awakening are you in?

Why did Albert Einstein say — "No problem can be solved from the same level of consciousness that created it"? *Because* **the only way to make all your problems disappear is to transcend them**. *(But how?)*

Popular bestselling author and star of the hit movie *The Secret*, Dr. Joe Vitale will take you on a magical journey through the four stages of awakening. Dr. Vitale will instruct you on the pitfalls and practices of each stage and will finally lead you into the fourth and final stage of complete awakening – a place RARELY described before. In the downloadable *Awakening Course*, you will learn...

- What it means to be awakened and why it's so important
- How you can **create your own awakened life filled with miracles**
- The steps to get out of the "victim" mentality
- Ways to TURN YOUR FEARS INTO CATALYSTS FOR SUCCESS
- How to move beyond ego
- **5 steps for attracting anything** or anyone into your life
- HOW THE UNIVERSE WORKS (the real truth)
- Cleaning and clearing methods allowing miracles
- How to re-state complaints into positive life-changing intentions
- The role gratitude plays in attracting what you want in your life
- How to **co-create with the Divine**
- A rare Hawaiian healing method and how you can use it to clean blocks
- Answers to questions on spirituality, ego, fear, children, and business

And more!

The downloadable *Awakening Course* (which downloads from the Internet – right into your computer) comes with 5 audio presentations, *Awakening Course* Live DVD, Inspired Action Guide and **TWO FREE BONUS audio presentations (Awakened Millionaire and Awakened Relationship)**! (ALL DOWNLOADABLE TO YOUR COMPUTER IN MINUTES.)

To learn more and order today, go to...

www.awakeningdownload.com

Listen to this – "The Secret to Attracting Money!"

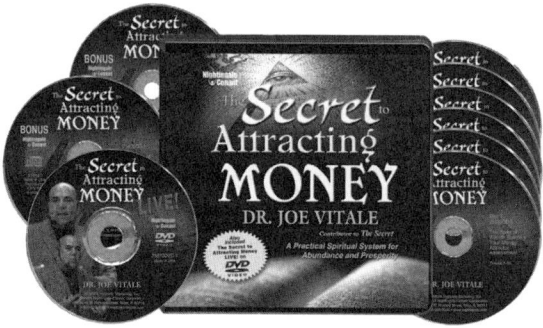

The potential to attract money and create abundant wealth doesn't reside in your job, your circumstances, or even the economy. **It resides within YOU.** Your mind is equipped with the natural ability to **attract as much money as you want and need** — at ANYTIME, ANYPLACE, in any financial climate, without struggle. **You just have to know how to trigger it.**

In this life-changing "abundance" program, self-made multimillionaire and *The Secret* co-star Dr. Joe Vitale shows you how to tap into the awesome force of the Law of Attraction, and focus it like a laser for one purpose — attracting more money into your life.

Dr. Vitale will show you empowering new thought processes that will open the floodgates to UNLIMITED MONEY AND WEALTH. You'll also learn how to:

- Attract money in any economy using a PROVEN 5-step economy-proof formula
- Reprogram your mind to **start attracting money right away**
- Avoid the lies, myths, and media conspiracies that will keep you in a state of "victimhood" and "poverty consciousness"
- Uncover compelling new reasons for wanting money that will **amplify your money-attraction powers**, allowing you to attract money & wealth easier and much faster than you can imagine
- Utilize Dr. Vitale's proven tips, insights and resources to help you attract money at lightning speed
- Create business and entrepreneurial opportunities, while doing what you love — by following a detailed, step-by-step plan

And so much more!

The Secret to Attracting Money comes with 6 CDs, 2 Bonus CDs, DVD, and interactive workbook. To learn more and order today, go to…

www.thesecrettoattractingmoney.com

Catalog of Products

Why haven't YOU attracted all the money you want? What's the real secret to removing hidden inner blocks so you can have more money ASAP?

"At last! - You can now **start clearing the unconscious limiting beliefs that have prevented your attracting all the money you desire**!"

The *Clearing MONEY Audio*™ is a BREAKTHROUGH IN PERSONAL GROWTH. It contains original music by Pat O'Bryan (an accomplished musician with several CDs released) and original statements by Dr. Joe Vitale, a certified hypnotherapist and "master belief cleanser."

The combination of spoken commands and original music, combined with some high-tech binaural sounds [Milagro VF™], creates a unique audio that speaks to your unconscious mind. The music is easy listening, relaxing, and de-stressing. You can play it while you work, drive, rest, exercise or even sleep. You can listen to it once a day, once every few days, or whenever you feel inspired to play it.

Order the *Clearing MONEY Audio*™ right now and you can download and listen to it on your computer, iPod or any other player.

To learn more and order today, go to...

www.clearingformoney.com

Like you, I hear about so many health products and read so many claims that most of it becomes a blur. And most of it isn't more than hype, anyway. So I'm as skeptical as anyone when it comes to the "latest thing," especially in the world of health.

But I keep an open mind, keep researching, take a handful of proven products myself, and stay hopeful that one day I'll find a new product that actually does what the marketing for it claims. If you (or someone you know) is interested in better health and/or anti-aging, this might be of real value. It might even be a life-saver. It might even be the Fountain of Youth.

It's called Youth Juice.

Youth Juice currently yields the highest ORAC value of *any* product on the market (12,350 per serving). In the world of anti-aging medicine, highest ORAC translates to highest anti-aging effects.

It contains 7 important antioxidant-loaded and cancer-fighting berries (raspberries, blueberries, blackberries, black elderberries, blackcurrant berries, boysenberries, and cranberries).

It also contains 3 immune-enhancing and detoxifying sea vegetables (fucoidan, rockweed, and ulva).

Rather than pretend I know what I'm talking about (I'm not a medical doctor, remember, though I am a member of the American Academy of Anti-Aging Medicine), just visit the site below for more information.

Again, I feel this is essential to good health. I take it myself. Get more details at...

http://ourworldnetwork.com/mrfire

What is *The Solution* to all Problems?

Dr. Joe Vitale goes beyond feel good pep talks to reveal the real solution to attracting miracles in EVERY area of your life and transcending your problems.

Inspiring, enlightening and mind expanding, Dr. Vitale's *The Solution* involves **a proven step-by-step methodology** to quickly get you out of what he calls "Victimhood."

The Solution reveals:

- How to break free from victim mentality - so you can get on with your life
- How to release limiting beliefs about money and relationships once and for all
- How to **release fear and find courage in every area of your life**
- How to go from goal "setting" to goal "getting" faster than you can imagine
- Three time-tested ways to ATTRACT MIRACLES in every area of your life
- The four-step path to true spiritual awakening
- Three words that are guaranteed to change your life (and the planet) forever

Discover *The Solution* today!

To learn more and order today, you can purchase at either iTunes or Audible.com below…

www.itunes.com

www.audible.com

Attract Miracles

"What Would Happen if 8,185 People Held an Intention for You Personally?"

FACT: 23 scientific studies PROVE that when groups of people meditate, the crime and violence in their area goes down

AND the wealth, peace, and prosperity goes up.

I'm creating a community of people to do just that – hold your intention (whatever it may be) FOR you – The combined energy of this number will virtually guarantee your results!

Think of what this would mean to your life, your family, your city, state and even the planet!

Read on to discover how to join this movement TODAY!

What kind of miracle are you looking for?

Whether it's love, healing, money, or anything else, wouldn't it be easier if you had help? Of course it would.

And that is the inspiration behind *The Attract Miracles Community*.

You get access to other members who can help you attract miracles — **guided meditations** to help you ATTRACT MIRACLES FASTER than ever — **personalized answers to your questions** — **new audio or video presentation every month** — **access to my "Miracles Library" of digital books** — **inspiring videos** — AND MUCH MORE!

You'll also get instant access to many of my courses, seminar audios & videos (and MORE will be added each month) including: *Zero Limits I* Audio Program, *Zero Limits II* Audio Program, *Breakthrough Manifestation Weekend* Audio Program, *Breakthrough Manifestation Weekend II* Audio Program, *Miracles Weekend in San Diego* Video Program and my exclusive *AAA Plan to Attracting Wealth* program.

Join *Attract Miracles* or learn more at...

www.attractmiracles.com

Activate the full power of the Law of Attraction using the critical "missing piece" that empowers you to automatically and consistently get what you want!

According to Dr. Joe Vitale, it's one thing to know what the Law of Attraction is. But if you want to put the power of this incredible natural force to work for you in a positive and consistent way, you MUST understand something else ... the "Missing Secret" that will bring it all together for you. In this wise, warm, and ultimately life-changing program, Joe Vitale uncovers what this missing component is, and shows you how to **use it to attract wealth, health, success, happiness, love, and more into your life** — quickly, consistently, and automatically.

In these 12 sessions you'll discover how to:

- **Turn ANY desire into reality, using the PROVEN 5-step Attractor Factor Process**
- Stop attracting what you don't want, by identifying and eliminating the subconscious beliefs that are bringing negative experiences into your life right now
- **Remove all your limitations and start living** and achieving at a level you never imagined possible before, using the revolutionary Self-Identity Ho'oponopono Process
- Begin to instantaneously HEAL injury, illness, disconnects, and more, using 4 simple phrases
- **Attract positive outcomes** into the lives of others — no matter how far away they are or how difficult their challenges may be

And so much more!

The Missing Secret comes with 6 CDs, *Install And Transcend The Secret* DVD, *The Missing Secret Progress Guide* and *Thought Vibration* book.

To learn more and order today, go to...

www.nightingale.com

ATTRACT MONEY *NOW!*

Be sure to pick up these other titles from Dr. Joe Vitale

   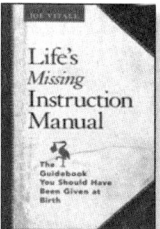 

Attractor Factor The Key Zero Limits Life's Missing Instruction Manual Seven Lost Secrets of Success

Inspired Marketing Hypnotic Writing Your Internet Cash Machine Meet & Grow Rich

There's A Customer Born Every Minute Spiritual Marketing Expect Miracles Buying Trances

ALL AVAILABLE AT

ABOUT THE AUTHOR

DR. JOE VITALE

Bestselling author Joe Vitale, is known as the world's ONLY "spiritual" marketer. Combining his unique, one-of-a-kind charismatic/inspirational style, and exclusive 7-step money "attraction" formula, Joe has successfully coached thousands of people, through his seminars, books, DVDs, webinars, and TV/radio appearances, on the "Law of Attraction." Testimonials from all over the world prove **Joe's formula for attracting wealth, health, love, and happiness work**. His system has helped countless people become millionaires and find happiness. Joe's system is so effective, he was asked to co-star in the world-famous movie *The Secret*, as well as contribute to the book. (He also starred in *The Leap*, *The Opus*, *Try It On Everything*, and his latest – *The Compass*.)

Joe Vitale developed his 7-step formula when he went from literally being homeless, living on the streets, to becoming one of the most prolific writers and entrepreneurs. Now he is financially independent living the life most only dream about. His life's mission is to help others to do the same.

As a writer, Joe Vitale has written many bestsellers on the "Law of Attraction" and marketing including...

- **Expect Miracles:** *The Missing Secret to Astounding Success*
- **Attract Money Now Hardcover Book**
- **The Key:** *The Missing Secret for Attracting Anything You Want*
- **The Attractor Factor (Second Edition):** *5 Easy Steps for Creating Wealth (or anything else)*

ATTRACT MONEY NOW!

- **Life's Missing Instruction Manual:** *The Guidebook You Should Have Been Given at Birth.*
- **Zero Limits:** *The Secret Hawaiian System for Wealth, Health, Peace, and More*
- **Spiritual Marketing:** *A Proven 5-Step Formula for Easily Creating Wealth from the Inside Out*
- **How to Attain Your Desires:** *How to Live Life And Love It*
- **How to Attain Your Desires by Letting Your Subconscious Mind Work for You**
- **Adventures Within:** *Confessions of an Inner-World Journalist*
- **The Seven Lost Secrets of Success**
- **At Your Command:** *The Famous Mystic's Universal Recipe for Guaranteed Success in Any Situation*
- **The Successful Coach:** *Insider Secrets to Becoming a Top Coach*
- **Your Internet Cash Machine:** *The Insider's Guide to Making Big Money, Fast!*
- **Hypnotic Writing:** *How to Seduce and Persuade Customers With Only Your Words*
- **Buying Trances:** *A New Psychology of Sales and Marketing*
- **Meet and Grow Rich:** *How to Easily Create and Operate Your Own "Mastermind" Group for Health, Wealth, and More*
- **There's a Customer Born Every Minute:** *P.T. Barnum's Secrets to Business Success*
- **The E-Code:** *32 Internet Superstars Reveal 47 Ways to Make Money Online Almost Instantly*
- **The Greatest Money-Making Secret in History!**
- **Cyber Writing: How to Promote Your Product or Service Online (Without Being Flamed)**
- **The A.M.A. Complete Guide to Small Business Advertising**
- **How to Write & Publish Your Own eBook in As Little as 7 Days**
- **How ANY Book Can Become an Amazon Bestseller!**

About the Author

Joe also is the founder of the *"Joe Vitale Miracles Coaching™ program."* This is the only program dedicated to teaching thousands of people, through one-on-one coaching, how to use the "Law of Attraction" to create miracles in their lives. He also is the founder of the *"Hypnotic Marketing Coaching program."* Here you can learn, through one-on-one mentoring, how to start and succeed in your own business.

Joe has also starred in and produced CD/DVD programs including...

- **The Secret to Attracting Money**
- **The Awakening Course:** Discover the Missing Secret for Attracting Health, Wealth, Happiness and Love
- **The Missing Secret Home Study Course:** How to Use The Law of Attraction to Easily Attract What You Want ... Every Time
- **The Missing Secret:** Lecture Series Volume 1&2
- **The Solution**
- **The Subliminal Manifestation Series — Forgiveness and Love**
- **The Subliminal Manifestation Series — Fear-Less:** Transcend and Break Through Fear
- **The Subliminal Manifestation Series — Accumulating Wealth:** Magnetizing Your Unconscious Mind for Prosperity
- **The Subliminal Manifestation Series — Increase Sales**
- **Dreaming Abundance**
- **The Attractor Factor Blueprint Essential DVD Study Course**
- **The Beyond Manifestation Spiritual Growth System**
- **Money Beyond Belief**
- **How to Attract A New Car**

Joe Vitale is a much sought-after public speaker, speaking to thousands of people annually at prestigious events including the Learning Annex expo and the National Speaker's Association among other large-scale events.

He's also one of the most sought-after media interviews. His most recent interviews include, *Larry King Live, The Big Idea With Donny Deutsch, Extra TV*, and *Newsweek* magazine.

Joe's website address is www.joevitale.com. Here, Joe presents all his products/services, speaking schedule, and links to his blog sites. Readers can also sign up for his mail list right on the homepage. Or, readers can subscribe to his *Awakening Monthly* newsletter at http://www.awakeningmonthly.com. He has also started a website community for people who want to attract miracles in their life called Attract Miracles at http://www.attractmiracles.com.

Joe Vitale is also a passionate philanthropist and humanitarian, working with many private and public organizations. Joe has even started his own charity to combat homelessness and foreclosures called Operation YES at http://www.operationyes.com.

For general information on Joe Vitale or his organization, Hypnotic Marketing, Inc., please contact his VP of Operations, Suzanne Burns, at 1-512-278-1610, or you may e-mail her at Suzanne@mrfire.com.

WWW.JOEVITALE.COM

GET THE BOOK!

✓ Hard Cover Book

For printed hardcover copies of this book – to give to family, friends, schools, hospitals, churches, groups, wards, etc.
– or just to carry to the beach or on a plane –
See http://www.attractmoneynowbook.com/

SPECIAL MIRACLES COACHING™ OFFER!

For the past 25 years I've been helping people like you attract ALL kinds of miracles in EVERY area of their lives.

I've helped people attract...
Money • Cars • Soul Mates • Better Health
New Careers • Dream Homes

The list goes on and on! And I can help you do the same in my new *Joe Vitale's Miracles Coaching™ program!* The key is for you to be ready. (And it looks like you are or you would not be reading *Attract Money Now*.) If you want to learn more about how you can attract money, jobs, health, love, careers, relationships or anything else quickly, and you want to sign up now, just go to…

www.miraclescoaching.com